Oh-h-h! those '56 OLDSMOBILES!

with new *Jetaway* HYDRA-MATIC

ALL THE *Flow* OF FLUID ... ALL THE *Go* OF GEARS!

ADS
That Put
AMERICA ON WHEELS

Eric Dregni & Karl Hagstrom Miller

Motorbooks International
Publishers & Wholesalers ®

ACKNOWLEDGMENTS

Thanks to Stacey Becklund, Car Henge, the *City Pages* newspaper, Juan Dicus, Jay Dregni, John Dregni, Michael Dregni, Amy Hagstrom Miller, Danny· Walkowitz and the Identity Boys, Steve Hanson, Hungry Mind Book Emporium, Zack Miller, Mary Tyler Marx, Thurston Moore's angry rock grimaces, Rossini's *Barbiere di Siviglia*, Meredith Sommers, Sven the Cat, and of course Vinnie & the Stardüsters.

First published in 1996 by Motorbooks International Publishers & Wholesalers, 729 Prospect Avenue, PO Box 1,Osceola, WI 54020-0001

© Eric Dregni, Karl Hagstrom Miller, 1996

Motorbooks International books are also available at discounts in bulk quantity for industrial or sales-promotional use. For details write to Special Sales Manager at the Publisher's address

Library of Congress Cataloging-in-Publication Data

Dregni, Eric
    Ads that put America on wheels / Eric Dregni, Miller, Karl Hagstrom.
        p.   cm.
    Includes index.
    ISBN 0-7603-0137-9 (pbk. : alk. paper)
    1. Advertising—Automobiles—United States—History—20th century.
    2. Automobile industry and trade—United States—History—20th century.   I. Miller, Karl Hagstrom 1968- . II. Title.
    HF6161.A9D74 1996
    659.1'96292'092730904—dc20   96-24918

On the front cover: Computer enhancement of 1961 Plymouth ad. *Rick Schunk*

Printed in Hong Kong

★ ★ ★   ★ ★ ★

CONTENTS

The Lincoln Cosmopolitan Convertible. White side-wall tires and road lamps optional at extra cost.

If you want a fine car that is one in a million, not like a million others...then you may drive the great new 1949 Lincoln Cosmopolitan anywhere, in any company, safe in the assurance you are driving the most distinctive fine car on the road. Lincoln Division of Ford Motor Company.

Lincoln makes America's Most Distinctive Cars

"YOU CAN'T GET TO TOWN IN A TUB"

"We just have to have cars. A car is no longer just a family necessity but is an individual, personal necessity. We can't get along without cars . . ."
—*1958 Rambler ad*

"You can't get to town in a tub," declared a Muncie, Indiana, woman when asked by sociologists Robert and Helen Lynd in 1929 why she chose to buy a car rather than indoor plumbing. She may just as well have answered that no one can see you enjoying your new tub, but the right car can make you the talk of the town. From their earliest days, automobiles have embraced style as well as transportation. They get you where you need to go. Yet at the same time they are rolling advertisements for the driver, telling everyone in eye- and earshot just what kind of character is pumping the pedal. Or so advertisers would have us believe. The hunks of steel that fill the nation's garages, streets and even National Parks are the products of automobile manufacturers. They are not, however, the only ones responsible for America's long love affair with the car. While many of the bodies come from the assembly lines in Detroit, many of the dreams and ideas we have about what the automobile is and should be come straight from Madison Avenue. This is the story of how advertisers helped sell America on the automobile.

At the turn of the century the car was a plaything of the ultrarich, but by the time of the Lynds' study it had become a necessity. In a few short decades, the automobile revolutionized American transportation. Millions put their horses out to pasture and rejected the regulation of the trolley car, opting instead for the freedom (if not the reliability) of their new autogos, autocycles, and zent-, pneu-, and far-mobiles. Hundreds of car manufacturers popped up—most were reputable, but many were fly-by-night operations ready to cash in on the new horseless carriage fad.

Hopping behind the tiller or wheel of an early car was a dirty, unsafe, and often all too adventurous experience. Open-air cabs meant drivers' faces were full of dust, grime, and engine fumes. Service stations were few and far between, meaning motorists with broken-down cars had to regularly

Convertibles!
This 1949 Lincoln was perfect for cruising around sunny California, or anywhere with poolside motels. A 1937 Chrysler ad bragged about their convertibles as "alive with the spirit of youth . . . flair in every line. Squeak proof . . . rattle proof . . . quiet as a closed car! Tops that fold like magic . . . completely out of sight!"

Bathtub Car
The 1949 Nash was known for its bathtub styling, allowing happy owners to drive to town in a tub. This Airflyte Nash had reclining seats forming its "Twin Convertible Beds." Years before seat belts came into use, Nash offered them as optional equipment, although not to protect the passengers in a crash, but to hold them in place while sleeping in the car.

Meet the No.1 PEOPLE of Hudson Town!

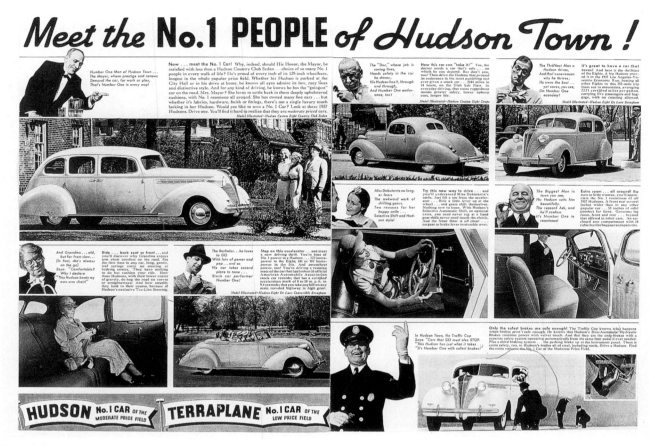

Up with People!
Advertisements were filled with images of the public as ad agents imagined them. They may all have been different but they each had problems that could only be solved by a new car—preferably a 1937 Hudson. *Steve Hanson Collection*

rely on old-fashioned horsepower for a tow. Dirt roads were unkind to the new contraptions and sucked harder than the La Brea Tar Pits once the rains came.

Early automobile owners didn't give a damn about any of this. After all, they didn't always drive to *get* somewhere—they drove to *be* somebody. In the first decade of the century, a Pierce-Arrow cost as much as a fully furnished six-room house. Even though gas was in some places cheaper than oats, the high initial investment barred car ownership to all but the wealthy. The wallets of the rich overflowed into huge sculptures of leather and steel. Cars spoke not of necessity but style, character, and conspicuous consumption.

Enter the advertisers. The modern advertising industry grew out of two earlier traditions. The same years that saw the rise of American automobility witnessed the growth of crude 19th-century ad placement services into what insiders liked to consider a respectable industry. Early advertising agencies had no graphic artists, copywriters, or

designers. They consisted of middlemen who, for a fee, would arrange the purchase of ad space in newspapers and magazines. How customers filled that space was not the agency's responsibility. From the 1890s through the 1910s, advertisers, like many members of the burgeoning professional sector, became more complex and specialized in the services they provided. Agencies slowly began to make layout and copy suggestions to the customers who came to them attempting to improve sales of their sewing machines, beauty supplies, and anything else under the sun. Eventually they featured these extra services and began hiring staff who specialized in different aspects of ad creation.

The second wellspring of modern advertising was the traveling salesman of yore. The itinerant huckster would pull his flashy wagon into a town and set up shop. In front of a crowd of curious onlookers he would preach the benefits of his newfangled miracle medicine. Someone who was lame, bald, or just lacking that vital pep would (with a knowing wink to the salesman) down a

Ad That Could Only Sell Cars to Taxi Companies
Checker started making taxi cabs in the 1920s. From 1959 and into the 1980s, it also offered cars to the general public. Some considered Checkers to be modern classics, because of the fact that their design never changed much. But few "civilian" Checkers were ever sold, due in part to poor gas mileage, which made them most practical for driving between gas stations.

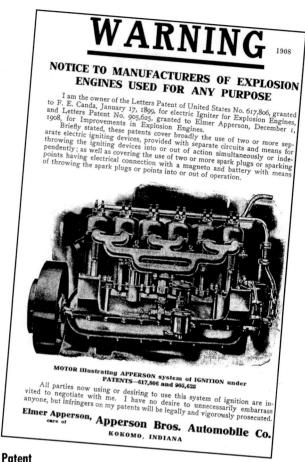

Patent Infringement?
Elmer Apperson could have made a million if everyone would have paid to use his ignition system. In an effort to gain royalties, inventors tried to patent many things—including the internal combustion engine. Fortunately, variations in engine design allowed manufacturers to skirt sometimes spurious patents and put an auto in every garage.

jigger of the fabulous fluid and be instantly cured. Suckers would fork over their money, and the salesman would be in the next town before anyone was the wiser. Perhaps the greatest 19th-century purveyor of this tradition was P. T. Barnum. Barnum started his career as a patent-medicine salesman, and he got rich selling fantasies and humbugs to people, most of whom, he said, "appear disposed to be amused even when they are conscious of being deceived." In 1842, he plastered New York City with posters promoting the beautiful mermaid on display at his museum. After the droves paid their 25 cents admission they encountered nothing but a fish tail sewn to the body of a dried monkey. People kept coming, however, content in their newfound knowledge that advertisements were goofy exaggerations—good for a laugh but not to be taken very seriously.

Early in the 20th century, advertisers and ad agencies were hopelessly embarrassed by their asso-

ciation with the huckster tradition. They did everything possible (except quitting the business) to distance themselves from their disreputable predecessors. They wore expensive suits and set up fancy offices. They developed a pseudoscientific language to give their profession some cachet. They attended the opera. Nothing, however, granted self-respect quicker than the growing notion that advertising was selling products that would better people's lives. Advertising, its practitioners believed, was helping to bring the masses up to speed, pulling them out of their tired 19th-century ways into the vital, fast-paced, and efficient world of 20th-century mass production. Purveyors of advertising figured themselves, in historian Roland Marchand's term, "disciples of modernity."

Auto manufacturers similarly considered themselves apostles of the new. The two industries rode each other's coattails to prominence. Car ownership skyrocketed following the spread of

FLORIDA HIGHLIGHTS

SKETCHED IN AND AROUND MIAMI BY FLOYD DAVIS

THE NATION'S SOCIAL CAPITAL moves South. And social leaders, seeking rest, find Florida's season the gayest since 1929.

• • •

MIAMI'S SPORTING CALENDAR is studded with sailing events, which reach their height in the annual St. Petersburg Race.

THERE'S STILL NO EQUAL TO THE MOTORING THRILL OF DE SOTO'S AIRFLOW

Two years ago, De Soto introduced the famous Airflow car. Today, its scientific weight distribution...equalized springing...seating for six...are still the most talked-about features in cars. And many are the efforts to copy them.

Spend a few minutes with De Soto's Airflow III. Feel the utter relaxation of travel that's silent, swift and sure. Test the economy of its Gas-Saver Transmission. See its custom-styled interiors...the new beauty of its extended front and modern, streamlined trunk. America's lowest-priced Airflow is still *years* ahead! Sedan or coupe, $1095, list at factory, Detroit. Special equipment extra. Ask for new 6% Time Payment Plan.

DE SOTO
Product of the Chrysler Corporation

Airflow **III**

COMPANION CAR TO AIRSTREAM DE SOTO

DANCING AT THE DEAUVILLE...and revealing the mode in wide-cut evening frocks. Slippers in vivid reds, greens, blues are quite the thing this season.

YACHTSMAN CARTER says of De Soto Airflow III—"Every car should have De Soto's safety...genuine hydraulic brakes, steel unit frame-and-body."

FORD THUNDERBIRD '59

The car everyone would love to own!

Hard Sell
Scripted by either a lazy or concise copywriter, this ad for the 1959 Thunderbird plainly states the joy of possession. By the mid-1950s 87 percent of American families owned a car, and 52 percent owned more than one. Such abundance gave us not only crowded streets but beautiful, pollution-hazed sunsets like this one.

Streamline Moderne
Left: Edsel wasn't the first car flop to hit the market. The avant-garde 1934 Chrysler Airflow and this 1936 DeSoto Airflow III, with 40 percent less air resistance and eight cylinders, was far too advanced for its time. Airflows were dropped in 1937 and their failure pushed Chrysler into the most conservative posture of America's "Big Three" carmakers.

Tin Lizzie fever and the 1921 rebirth of General Motors. A prosperous economy put more disposable income in people's pockets and made purchasing an automobile a new possibility for millions. In 1920, there was one car registered in the United States for every three households. Nine years later there was one for every 1.2 households, and new vehicle sales surpassed the 5-million-unit mark. Carmakers increased their advertising budgets apace with their automobile production. During the decade, auto companies became the advertising industry's biggest clients. In the course of only four years, from 1923 to 1927, automakers pumped up their advertising expenditures from

$3.5 million to $9.3 million. In the process they transformed a luxury item into a product many could not do without.

The 1920s also were the decade in which the advertising profession came into its own, greatly aided by big-buck car clients. Landing a major auto account could catapult a minor agency to the big leagues, and even today ad firms flaunt their car campaigns like hard-won merit badges. The nation's economic prosperity coming out of the 1921 recession allowed people to buy more than just automobiles, and advertising gained new power as the front guard in the transition from a mass-production to a mass-consumption society. Advertising, more than any time before or since, could lead public taste and create a demand for a product, rather than reflect that which was already there. To a large extent, those who made ads tried to cast the masses in their own image. As historian Jackson Lears argues, the people in advertisements looked like advertising executives—they lived in above-average homes, worked at white-collar jobs, constantly worried about their appearance, and spent their evenings at fancy parties rather than movie theaters. When consumers were pictured in ads they did not appear as they did in real life but as advertisers imagined them to be. In this way, advertising sold more than a new automobile. It sold a lifestyle. Many Americans were more than happy to sign on the dotted line and purchase their way to a better world.

Over the following decades, the advertising industry learned to get off its pedestal and meet the consumer halfway. Advertisements became less high-brow and reflected that not everyone wanted to don evening wear and hire a chauffeur. But true to its huckster roots, advertising still professed that a new car could change one's life. The makers of automobiles and automotive advertising developed a vast number of ways to sell automobiles to the American public. They pitched products any way they could think of to make a sale. If one idea didn't work, they would try another. Some were self-righteous, others downright silly. They used status and sex, technological innovation and style, visions of the future and nostalgia for the past.

This book charts the various advertising messages and methods that have been used—each one, believe it or not, the result of countless hours of preparation. Each ad, no matter how beautiful or ridiculous, was created with one purpose in mind: to get you in the driver's seat of a new dream machine.

So buckle up, check your rearview mirror, and take a winding trip through the ads that put America on wheels. ■

The Thunderbird Touch:
A Stereo-Tape System…Highway Pilot Control…
Overhead Safety Control Panel

Thunderbird Town Hardtop

This is Thunderbird 1966! **A new Stereo-Tape System** is but one of many exclusive options. It surrounds you with music from four high-fidelity stereo speakers.

Highway Pilot Control is another. Mounted at your fingertips, within the spokes of the steering wheel, Highway Pilot lets you set, retard, and resume your cruising speed at the touch of a button.

And the Overhead Safety Control Panel, standard on Town Landau and Town Hardtop models, has lights to remind you if fuel is low, a door ajar, or to fasten seatbelts—and an Emergency Flasher that sets four exterior lights blinking. Thunderbird 1966 will touch your driving with total luxury. Drive one today.

Thunderbird

UNIQUE IN ALL THE WORLD

TECHNOLOGY

Early automotive entre-preneurs probably had little idea their work would be the seed for future sedans, convert-ibles, town cars, and sta-tion wagons, not to mention the consequent redesigning of cities and streets, and the creation of highways designed for cars.

Sometimes through necessity, but usually for convenience, car manufacturers have continually tried to reinvent the automobile, if not the wheel. Early on, such efforts ranged from the self-starter, designed in the 1910s as a "ladies aid," to automatic transmissions, which first appeared around 1937.

America's entry into World War II brought a temporary cessation to the production of new cars, but not of new ideas. When hostilities ended, the American auto industry had the wherewithal to make cars and trucks that were like nothing seen before, and American consumers were ready to buy as never before. Detroit responded with powerful new engines, new comfort and conve-nience features, enhanced safety, and most signifi-cantly, with looks that contrasted sharply with those of the prewar Depression era, when cars typ-ically had all the excitement of sensible shoes.

What was under the hood continued to be important, but no more so than the hood itself.

Overhead Orchestra
While this 1966 T-Bird had a state-of-the-art hi-fi, next year's model came with a "Stereo-Sonic Tape System," which was an eight-track tape player. Even so, four-way hi-fi could hardly be ignored. Meanwhile, the Ford Mustang of the era invited customers to assemble their own cars from its huge option list, often causing customers to spend almost as much on extras as on the basic car.

"Ford Family of Fine Cars"
Next page: The 1932 Model B V-8 put Ford back in the game following a lull in sales due to its insistence on staying with the four-cylinder Model T and Model A for years after they were out of date. "They give you more *usable* horsepower . . . more torque—the engineer's word for wheel-turning power. . . . This, we believe, is the new kind of power that today's Americans want," read the text from this 1956 Ford ad.

"Hydra-Matic Drive has been thoroughly owner-proved in billions of miles of driving. And it was thoroughly battle-proved, during the war, in thousands of Army tanks."
—1946 Oldsmobile ad

Styling was the end-all sales pitch for the 1950s. The taller the fins, the more daring the driver; the more tones and chrome, the more inter-esting and rich the owner. The sales pitch for the 1953 Oldsmobile boasted of its 52 pounds of chrome.

The 1960s were a decade of change. As they dawned, the Big Three still had a corner on the market, but thanks to cars like the Volkswagen Beetle, younger consumers had begun to wonder if Detroit really had all the answers. Bigger wasn't necessarily better, and what about quality and value? Had American cars become too bloated to offer really significant performance?

Ironically, when American carmakers were just beginning to feel formidable competition from outside, old-fashioned homegrown ingenuity helped save the day. John DeLorean, then Pontiac's advanced engineering boss, had seen Detroit kids drag racing on Woodward Avenue. Many had put big V-8 engines into relatively small domestic cars, like the Pontiac's own Tempest. DeLorean saw a potential sales gold mine and ordered the develop-ment of the 1964 Pontiac GTO. "GTO" was a des-ignation for a category of racing sports cars in which Ferraris were then dominant. In this case, GTO was used to suggest that Pontiac's inspiration might have been European. But all anyone really noticed was that this GTO was fast, thanks to the triple carburetor, 389-cubic-inch V-8 that Pontiac had shoehorned into a relatively small and light Tempest body. Pontiac's GTO was an immediate success, and soon "factory" hot-rodded cars were in showrooms everywhere. Ads pushed the power of "Advanced Thrust" with "explosive new go."

American muscle had once again put the U.S. automobile industry back into the game with cars like the Mach I Mustang, Mercury Cougar Eliminator, Ply-mouth Road Runner (with optional 426-cubic-inch Hemi engine), and, of course, the Pontiac GTO. ■

1. The FORD THUNDERBIRD   2. The CONTINENTAL MARK II

THE BIG TRENDS BEGIN AT FORD A NEW BREED

You hear a lot about V-8 engines these days—but there's a big difference in V-8's. The fact is that more have been built by the Ford Motor Company than by any other manufacturer, and out of this long experience has come a new breed of V-8 engines.

You find this new breed of engines in all the Ford Family of Fine Cars. They give you more *usable* horsepower —where it counts. They give you more torque—the engineer's word for wheel-turning power. You can feel this

surge underfoot—not only all the way up from zero miles an hour, where you do 90% of your driving, b the way up to the top speeds that take you away from da

This, we believe, is the new kind of power that to Americans want. And it typifies the new kind of given to you by the entire Ford Family of Fine Cars lowest-priced cars in the line, for example, have power than the costliest cars of yesterday. Becaus Ford Motor Company has spent so much time in rese

The MERCURY MONTCLAIR   4. The FORD FAIRLANE   5. The LINCOLN PREMIERE

NGINES NOW MOVES AMERICA

d experiment, the engines throughout the line are
:hter and more efficient, designed to give you more
 wer out of every drop of gasoline.

And each car in the family has improvements made
 ssible by the wide range of the line, and by the many
 Terent car *ideas* in the line. New safety advances, for
 ample, are on every car from the Ford to the Continental.

And so, more and more of today's people turn to this
new kind of value. One proof: today both the Ford and
the Mercury lead their respective classes in trade-in
value.

In short, the men of Ford build a new kind of value for
a new kind of people: the growing, restless people of mid-
century America. In fact, the Big Trends begin at Ford.

HE FORD FAMILY OF FINE CARS   FORD · THUNDERBIRD · MERCURY · LINCOLN · CONTINENTAL

THEY SHOO HORSES, DON'T THEY?

"She can tell what a sassy pony that's a cross between greased lightning and the place where it hits, can do with eleven hundred pounds of steel and action when he's going high, wide and handsome. The truth is—the Playboy was built for her."
—*1923 Jordan Playboy ad*

★   ★   ★

Although automobiles may have challenged trains, bicycles, and two feet as means of transportation, the real war was with horses. Cars were viewed as sanitary alternatives to the piles of manure—often six inches deep—covering city streets. Tuberculosis and yellow fever were attributed to the rising dust from dried dung, and attempts to wash the streets usually ended with stinking puddles and pedestrians plugging their noses.

The First Auto Ad
Although *Scientific American* ran cover stories of zeppelin highways crisscrossing the country, in this 1898 Winton Motor Carriage ad they unwittingly ushered in the dawn of the auto age. Early cars were designed with the engine in back to make them appear like true "horseless carriages."

New Willys Six
As though wild horses were under the hood, this 1930 Willys of Toledo, Ohio, even included blurry speed lines on the side of the car to show its speed. Since horses could only be bred to be so fast and powerful, automobiles' endless improvements were much welcomed.

65 HORSEPOWER
...72 MILES AN HOUR

PRICES START AT $695

Complete line of body types, $695 to $850.
Prices f. o. b. Toledo, O., and specifications
subject to change without notice.

Willys Six
Sedan De Luxe
$850

Horses would frequently die from old age or overexertion, causing horrible traffic jams. The corpses often wouldn't be moved for days since this was a fairly regular occurrence in major cities. Clay McShane reports in *Down the Asphalt Path* that in 1880, New York City had to dispose of 15,000 dead horses.

The automobile may have caused different kinds of pollution, but it was viewed in its early days as a godsend. Rarely were horses and buggies privately owned by urban dwellers, as that would require a stable both at home and at work. Even if they owned horses, urbanites rarely rode them, due to the animals' smell as well as the owners' fear of a horse being stolen when left tied. More often, people would jump on a carriage for a taxi, or a horse-pulled omnibus. Omnibuses could be replaced with sleighs at the first snowfall, a decided advantage over the ski-less auto. Unfortunately, horses often couldn't pull their loads in hilly cities like San Francisco, which led to that city's installation of "cable cars."

Horses posed numerous problems, but none greater than their lack of marketability. Horses could be sold on an individual basis, but they couldn't be standardized, mass-produced, and advertised like automobiles. Horse trading was an uncertain experience, so car manufacturers did their best to gloat over the disadvantages of horses, as in a 1926 Durant Motors ad that read "Without whip or goad or sweat or strain, the Star Car delivers great power."

Horses, however, continued to be a symbol of many things that Americans saw as positive. Thanks to the automobile, horses ceased to be an urban nightmare and it became easy to see them as a symbol of the free-spirited American West or, depending on the audience, as emblematic of wealth and good taste. In 1928 Packard ran an ad that pictured a man telling his son, "A fine car appeals to me as much as a good horse."

At the 1964 World's Fair, Ford introduced its soon-to-be extremely successful Mustang. Named after the P-51 Mustang airplane, but with a wild horse as its emblem, this car spawned a whole class of cars that would come to be known as "pony cars." Unfortunately, by 1971 the once sleek and light Mustang had grown into another too-big Detroit ride. As late as 1979, AMC invoked the equine image when

GANGWAY

FOR AMERICA'S FAVORITE !

Flying Horsepower

Breeze through summer—you've got Flying Horsepower. Your car surges up hills with power to spare—gives you smooth, economical driving on trip or in traffic! Fill up with Mobilgas Special—at the Sign of the Flying Red Horse!

Mobilgas Special

AMERICA'S FAVORITE !

SOCONY-VACUUM OIL CO., INC., and Affiliates: MAGNOLIA PETROLEUM CO., GENERAL PETROLEUM CORP.

Mobilgas
SOCONY-VACUUM

Horsefeathers!
Although bound for certain collision, the car would inevitably win, even against a Pegasus. Cars rapidly became the accepted form of transportation in the city where the density of horses had spread illnesses like hoof-and-mouth disease. Rural acceptance was slower in coming since stables were available and manure served as fertilizer.

the company ran an ad asking, "Why horse around?" which compared their Spirit to the Mustang.

The automobile won the battle on the highways, but the horse never lost its place in the hearts and minds of America. ∎

"I'm going to build a car for the masses," announced Henry Ford in 1903. Five years later, he introduced the Model T. Ford called it "the universal car" and it changed the face of America. In the early days, Ford rarely advertised. The T sold faster than Ford could make it thanks to plenty of word of mouth as well as publicity through the newspapers. U.S. President Theodore Roosevelt complained that Henry Ford got more publicity than he did in the Oval Office.

Ford was probably the most famous person of his age. To many he was a great equalizer; to *The New York Times* in 1928, he was "an industrial fascist—the Mussolini of Detroit." He was seen as a great hero in Russia, and Adolf Hitler even said, "I am a great admirer of his." Many of Ford's workers joked that Hitler had derived the idea of the Gestapo from the shift managers at the factories. Regardless of one's view, everyone agreed that he revolutionized mass-production and put an automobile within almost everyone's reach.

Ford focused little attention on chrome flourishes or redesigns of the T. Very few ads for the Model T were put into print since everyone already knew about this fantastic, affordable new tool. Who needed ads when the name of his product was already on every consumer's lips?

The Model T was preceded by the Model N, which achieved 45 miles per hour, got 20 miles per gallon, and cost under $600. Middle-class families could afford to drive it. But the Model T could be used by just about everyone for everything from transporting livestock to being hooked up to a circle saw and cutting boards. There was plenty of room under the wheels so the Tin Lizzie could trudge through the mud roads of the time.

THE NEW FORD CAR

An announcement of unusual importance to every automobile owner

by

HENRY FORD

FORD MOTOR COMPANY
Detroit, Michigan

Dash Oldsmobiles were being built. Facing a backlog of orders, Ransom E. Oldsmobile called on engineering genius Henry M. Leland, who came up with the assembly-line concept and thereby got Oldsmobile back on its feet. But it was the Model T that became known as "The Car that Put America on Wheels!" because Ford not only saw the assembly line as a means to make more cars, but also to put more people to work.

Although Ford was considered anti-union, he reduced the nine-hour daily grind to only eight, and in 1926 he proclaimed Saturday a day off. The latter probably wasn't due to early labor organizers, but rather because he wanted workers to have leisure time to take holiday outings (and of course to buy a Model T to get out of town). He wielded so much power that he knew other factories and businesses would have to follow suit, making the whole country head to the lake for the weekend or a picnic outing.

All good things must end, but Henry Ford refused to believe that the bottom had fallen out of the market for his universal car. He lowered the T's price to $290 in 1926 and increased the number of dealerships, 70 percent of which lost money. On May 26, 1927, when production of the Model T ceased, 15 million had been produced, a number unsurpassed until the little Volkswagen Beetle came along.

The idea of mass production didn't actually start with the Model T. As early as 1896, the Duryea Motor Wagon Company of Springfield, Massachusetts, was making cars to a single pattern. Duryea ultimately wasn't successful, but the process it pioneered was a step up from the hundreds of home workshops around the country trying their hands at cars in the 1890s. The birth of the assembly-line vehicles came about after a 1901 fire destroyed the factory where the already-popular Curved

Now came the hard part. Henry Ford kept his creditors at bay while he sank $250 million into the retooling of his factories to produce the Model A. Looking over at the successful Chevrolet factory, which William Knudsen had set up to change models every few years, one of the Ford execs said the company needed to "get rid of all the Model T sons of bitches . . . get away from the Model T methods of doing things." The Model A kept Ford alive, but wasn't nearly the runaway success that the T had been.

FACTORIES: THE CONSTANT UPGRADING OF PRODUCT

While Henry Ford may have advanced the concept of mass production, it was General Motor's Alfred Sloan who perfected it. By the 1930s, GM's assembly lines could economically accommodate model changes every few years, while Ford's methods continued to make model changes cumbersome and exorbitantly expensive.

In the 1920s, Sloan initiated what some would call "planned obsolescence." Sloan called it "constant upgrading of product," which he saw as the key to creating interest in buying a new car. There was no reason that mass-production technology couldn't have some pizzazz, so in 1927 Sloan hired Harley J. Earl to head up GM's styling department, which was then known as the "Art and Colour Section" of the Fisher Body Division. Chrysler soon followed suit, making Virgil Exner, Earl's counterpart, chief designer. By the early 1950s, styling was deemed more important than new engineering.

VICTORY is our Business

GM GENERAL MOTORS

Old Hands at new Jobs

PACKARD

Only where talent and industry are rewarded, can the highest standard of quality craftsmanship be maintained

This is Getting Personal!
While the 1929 Packard ad featured a Romanesque esthetic, Studebaker and GM are showing how down-home they can get. In the 1920s, who wanted their car built by some impersonal machine?

America's finest automotive craftsmen —many of them father-and-son teams —protect your new car investment by building long-lasting high quality into the amazing new 1947 Studebaker Champions and Commanders. The Molnars, Joseph, Frank and Steven, pictured above, comprise a typical family group—with a total of 65 Studebaker years to their credit.

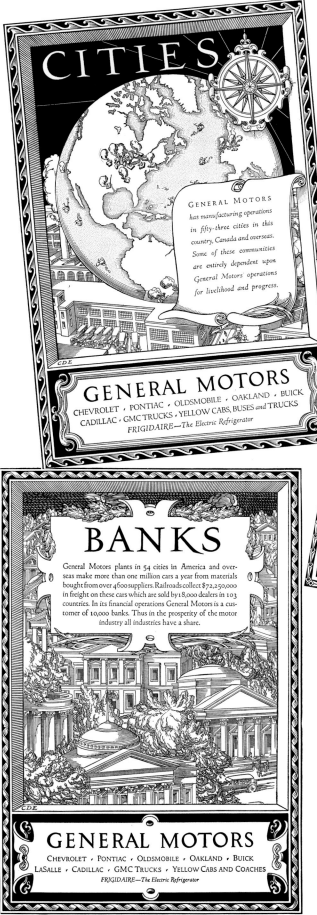

GM Rules the World

Alfred Sloan was appalled by what he saw as the dictatorial rule of Henry Ford and Walter Chrysler. GM was more decentralized and became the model for other corporations such as Standard Oil and Sears as they tightened their grip on the market. These 1927 ads show the GM oligarchy slowly taking over the world, a sentiment that then-GM President Charles Wilson would echo in 1953 with his infamous line, "What's good for the country is good for General Motors, and what's good for General Motors is good for the country."

The public continued to be awed by the huge corporations pumping out these beautiful machines, so ads regularly featured factories. Studebaker pushed its father-son teams concept during the war and postwar: Junior fought the bad guys while Pop made the machines to make it all possible. Fathers would take on their sons as apprentices when they got back from the war. "They get 'em young and train 'em right at Studebaker," claimed a 1946 ad. Meanwhile, Ford and Chrysler stressed the technology found in their factories. A 1945 Ford ad bragged, "Invisible rays, with frequencies millions of times greater than the highest frequency radio wave, now do the paint drying at Ford Motor Company." Chrysler showed a couple of execs peering godlike over a mini model of their factory claiming, "It took *imagination* to think of using toy-size model machines. . . ." GM went the scientific route in 1953, since everyone respects men in lab coats and gas masks fiddling around with large machines. "It is a far cry from the old-fashioned foundry to this block-long ultra-modern experimental metals laboratory at the new General Motors Technical Center."

GM, however, changed its tune in 1967 and decided to get personal, showing expert engineer Jim Rennel ruining engines: "he's murder on motors. For your protection." Compare that with an early 1904 Brew-Hatcher Co. of Cleveland, Ohio, ad claiming it performed "thorough tests on the road in the hands of ordinary users, not factory experts."

The factories continued to be upgraded. Sometimes improvements were advertised, other times they were hushed. Union skirmishes or adopting a Japanese system, like *kanban-jidoka*, don't always lend themselves to good ad copy—at least not the way computers do. The miracle of computer technology, or CAE, CAD and CAM (Computer-Aided Engineering, Design and Manufacturing), has become an advertising and business mainstay. ■

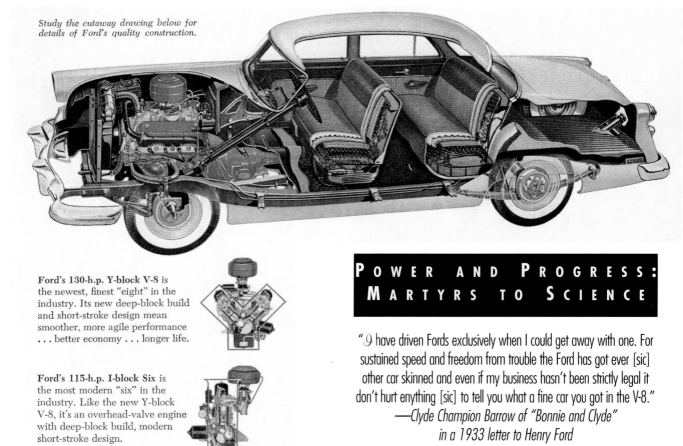

Study the cutaway drawing below for details of Ford's quality construction.

Ford's 130-h.p. Y-block V-8 is the newest, finest "eight" in the industry. Its new deep-block build and short-stroke design mean smoother, more agile performance . . . better economy . . . longer life.

Ford's 115-h.p. I-block Six is the most modern "six" in the industry. Like the new Y-block V-8, it's an overhead-valve engine with deep-block build, modern short-stroke design.

1954 Ford
Cutaways have always been popular advertising devices. Sometimes showrooms would display an actual car cut lengthwise in two to draw attention to all the spectacular features. This 1954 Ford came either with a 115-horsepower I-block Six or a 130-horsepower Y-Block V-8 both with special Fordomatic automatic drive with the " 'GO' of an automatic intermediate gear." A couple of years later, a Ford V-8 ad would rave that, "These engines pass in a wink with 'whoosh' in reserve."

POWER AND PROGRESS: MARTYRS TO SCIENCE

"*I* have driven Fords exclusively when I could get away with one. For sustained speed and freedom from trouble the Ford has got ever [sic] other car skinned and even if my business hasn't been strictly legal it don't hurt enything [sic] to tell you what a fine car you got in the V-8."
—*Clyde Champion Barrow of "Bonnie and Clyde"
in a 1933 letter to Henry Ford*

★   ★   ★

As soon as a second car was assembled, a race inevitably ensued. Automobiles blasted through streets at the unheard of speed of 20 miles per hour, as desperate mounted policeman were forced to shoot out tires to stop them. In 1906, cops in Cleveland were even ordered to stop using their pistols to stop speeders. Even so, a 1908 Black Motor Runabout ad pushed drivers onward, "Speed! I Guess Yes! . . . Travels any road—up hills through mud. 2 to 25 miles per hour. 30 miles on one gallon of gasoline."

FORD V·8

Happy Days Ahead

The Ford V-8 is an invitation to enjoy many thousands of miles of motoring. For the mother in the home. The young woman in business. The June Bride. And the girl graduate who has been longing for a car of her own. . . . For the purchase of a Ford V-8 is in itself something of a graduation—a step upward to a higher plane of motor car performance and all-around satisfaction. . . . Formerly you had to pay more than $2000 for a car with a V-8 engine. The Ford has brought it within your reach at a low price. And provided beauty, comfort, safety and richness of upholstery and appointment to match that fine car performance. . . . The Ford V-8 is thoroughly modern throughout. It stands at the head of its class in everything that means top honors for a motor car.

The Ideal Getaway Car
Ford may have pushed the 1935 V-8 for the "June Bride," but in reality, the V-8 was the notorious crime mobile. Both John Dillinger and Clyde Barrow (of Bonnie and Clyde) wrote to Henry Ford singing its praises as the best car to steal. Bonnie and Clyde may not have died if they had traded their 1934 Ford V-8s for the armor-plated McFarland favored by Al Capone. *Steve Hanson Collection*

Air Born B-58
Many ads featured all-out engine worship; a 1955 Chevrolet ad simply pictured an enormous engine block. This Air Born B-58 claimed "it looks and feels like flight on wheels."

Powerful way to go easy

Put yourself behind the wheel of a B-58 Buick and feel a completely new experience in driving. For here is power deliberately provided for your well-being and safety—power more than ample to handle easily any road situation you may meet. And with this power a new performance born of Flight Pitch Dynaflow* that can switch the pitch a million ways. You've never before sensed such immediate response and effortless ease. See your Buick dealer *today*.

BUICK *Division of* GENERAL MOTORS

Flight Pitch Dynaflow standard on LIMITED and ROADMASTER 75, optional at extra cost on other Series. Buick air ride optional at extra cost on all Series. Aluminum Front Brakes standard on all Series except SPECIAL.

The unique **OPEL** — The imported car made by General Motors in Germany—can now be ordered in Sedan and Caravan Wagon models through authorized Buick dealers.

NOW—more than ever—When better automobiles are built Buick will build them

Every window of every Buick is SAFETY PLATE Glass.

Try the **B-12,000 ENGINE** *it puts 12,000 pounds of thrust behind every piston stroke!*

It gives you the extra margin of safety of an engine that can deliver a sudden burst of needed power easily. It's the most modern engine possible to build for today's fuels.

☆

ONLY BUICK OFFERS YOU ALL THIS: Fresh Bold Styling with the Dynastar Grille • The Miracle Chassis plus Buick air ride • Flight Pitch Dynaflow with the instant flexibility of a million switches of pitch • Award-winning Air-Cooled Aluminum Brakes*—year's greatest braking advance — with smoother, surer control and longer life • "Velvet Wall" Sound Silencing

See TALES OF WELLS FARGO, Monday Nights, NBC-TV and THE PATRICE MUNSEL SHOW, Friday Nights, ABC-TV

the **AIR BORN B-58 BUICK**
It looks and feels like flight on wheels

Since then, engines have grown consistently in power, pushing land-speed records ever higher. Laws were passed to restrict cars' velocity—during the war and again in the 1970s due to petroleum shortages. But limits climbed incrementally higher as new safety features, wider roads, and higher-visibility highways made speed more viable.

Once Ford released its V-8 engine in 1932, power became a key selling point. Gangsters such as Dillinger and Bonnie and Clyde raved about this powerful engine for swift getaways. "For climbing the 'big ones' . . . and for extra power in a pinch—it's the sweetest, thriftiest 'eight' he's ever handled! And it *is*!" proclaimed a later 1949 Mercury ad.

"Hill-flatteners" became the catch-all phrase for these new powerful cars, as a 1955 Chevrolet ad proclaimed, "See that fine fat mountain yonder? You can iron it out, flat as flounder . . . and easy as whistling! Just point one of Chevrolet's special hill-flatteners at it (either the 162-h.p. 'Turbo-Fire V-8' or the 180-h.p. 'Super Turbo-Fire') . . . and pull the trigger! Barr-r-r-o-o-O-O-OOM! Mister, you got you a flat mountain!"

Ford offered its hates-to-stand-still look on the 1956 Ford Thunderbird "To go with its 'GO,' " whatever that's supposed to mean. Or as a 1955 Lincoln Capri ad pushed its speed agenda, "No jerk, no lag—just one unbroken sweep of power from zero to superhighway speed limits."

"Technology would conquer all" was the theme, and to achieve this state of nirvana, cars would have to be "Martyrs to Science" as a 1929 GM ad stated. The idea was that eventually cars would become one and the same as planes. "The Aviation Idea in an Automobile. *An all new high in spirit and responsiveness*—that's what you get in the new airplane-engineered Mercury! Like the newest modern planes, it's packed with vital power—actually *more power per pound* than ever before."

These visions of streets as runways, or launching pads for rocketlike cars, were pictured in ads in the 1960s as blurry backgrounds with the car in focus. "Hill-flatteners" had turned into rocket ships. ■

EDSEL: FLOP OF THE CENTURY

America first saw the Edsel on live national television when a driver turned the key and the engine wouldn't turn over. Ignoring this omen, Ford went on to spend more money promoting the doomed Edsel than on any product up to that time.

Ford began work on its top-secret "E car" in 1952. The Edsel was to be the car to rocket Ford sales and allow it to surpass GM and Chrysler.

Having been the most conservative car manufacturer with respect to styling, Ford chose one of its best designers, Roy A. Brown, Jr. (whose Lincoln Futura design was never put into production, but later became the Batmobile).

The car's debut was supposed to be heralded by 75 automobile writers saddling up their brand-new Edsels in Detroit and zooming them home across the country to their local Ford dealers. But at the designated day for departure, only 68 Edsels were ready. Another omen?

The clumsy moniker Edsel came after extensive market research and brainstorming by Ford's ad agency Foote, Cone, and Belding, with what was then the largest ad budget in history. More than 20,000 names were offered and then tossed. Instead, the Edsel got its name from the only son of Henry Ford. Ford had asked the poet Marianne Moore to wax poetically for their upcoming automobile. She suggested the names "Andante con Moto," "Pastelogram," "Utopian Turtletop," and "Mongoose Civique." Ultimately, it was "Edsel" that became synonymous with "total marketing flop," or as Jack Paar dubbed it, "an Oldsmobile sucking a lemon."

The Edsel lasted little more than two years and only 110,847 models hit the streets. Ford could barely give them away. Today, collectors search out this high-end Ford, and Edsels are proudly displayed at vintage auto shows across the country. ■

It shows them all what _new_ really means —outside, inside, and on the road!

Step into the 1958 Edsel and you'll soon find out where the excitement is this year. Drivers coming toward you spot that classic vertical grille a block away. And as you pass, they glance into their rearview mirrors for another look at this year's most exciting car.

On the open road, your Edsel is watched eagerly for the already-famous performance of its big, new V-8 Edsel Engine. And parked in front of your home, your Edsel always gets even more attention—because it always says a lot about you. It says you chose elegant styling, luxurious comfort and such exclusive features as Edsel's famous Teletouch Drive—only shift that puts the buttons where they belong, on the steering-wheel hub.

Your Edsel also means you made a wonderful buy. For all medium-priced cars, this one really new car is actually priced the lowest.* See your Edsel Dealer this week.

*Based on actual comparison of suggested retail delivered prices of the Edsel Ranger and similarly equipped cars in the medium-price field.

EDSEL DIVISION • FORD MOTOR COMPANY

Left: Edsel Citation 2-door Hardtop. Engine: the E-475, with 475 foot-pounds of torque, 10.5 to one compression ratio, 345 horsepower. Transmission: Automatic with Teletouch Drive. Suspension: Ball joint with optional air suspension. Brakes: self-adjusting.

Of all medium-priced cars, the one that's really new is the lowest-priced, too!

1958 EDSEL

They'll know you've _arrived_ when you drive up in an Edsel

Suburban Still Life with Edsel
Edsel wasn't the first car to flop. The avant-garde 1934 Chrysler Airflow, with 40 percent less air resistance and eight cylinders, was too advanced for its time. Its failure made Chrysler the most conservative of the Big Three after it was dropped in 1937. What made the Edsel such a _glorious_ bomb was the ads. The largest advertising budget in history was heaped on with ridiculous hype, like keeping all Edsels covered until their release date on September 4, 1957. Ad copy foretold, "Maybe you'll see some of these carriers loaded with covered cars on your roads in the next few days. If you do, you might call to mind what one of their drivers said before he started out . . . he said, plainly and forcibly: 'Man, would I like to have one of these.' "

The EDSEL LOOK is here to stay
—it has the new ideas next year's cars are copying!

Edsel dared to break out of the look-alike rut to bring you fresh, distinctive styling. And it's an open secret in Detroit—the Edsel look will be the most copied look next year. So Edsel is naturally worth more now when you buy it—and it's bound to bring you more when you finally trade it in. Yet you can actually buy an Edsel for less than fifty dollars over the price of V-8's in the Low-Priced Three.* And see for yourself how much

more you get. Swing in behind the wheel and start Edsel's powerful new engine. Shift with exclusive Teletouch Drive—just a fingertip touch at the steering-wheel hub. Then sit back in luxurious contour seats and enjoy Edsel's room and roadability, its smooth handling. This is the wonderful new way to drive. Why settle for less? See your Edsel Dealer.

EDSEL DIVISION • FORD MOTOR COMPANY

*Based on comparison of manufacturers' suggested retail delivered prices.

Less than fifty dollars difference between Edsel and V-8's in the Low-Priced Three

OPTIONS

Many standard features on cars today began as extravagant luxury items for the elite. The first automobile self-starter was used on the 1912 Cadillac and designated a "ladies aid" for women who couldn't crank start the engine and were tired of the limits of electric cars. Another feature of this Caddy was battery-operated lighting rather than old-fashioned and inefficient gas lighting.

Slowly, such features ran the course from being optional devices for "delicate women" to becoming standard features for men demanding the same amenities. Vanity mirrors, heating, air-conditioning, and automatic transmissions eventually came stock on many cars. Padded upholstery—including the coveted Levi's edition of the AMC Gremlin—became common features on even the roughest, toughest pickups.

Henry Ford dragged his feet in the race for style in cars, believing instead that they should be practical forms of transport—at least until GM's designer Harley Earl started such a sales landslide that Ford had to follow suit. As a result, a 1934

Copycats?

It is highly unlikely that *any* other manufacturer will impersonate the Edsel ever. Of course other manufacturers did stumble, including AMC's adoption of the name "Pacer," which was the name of the least expensive Edsel.

Look. A lot more Chevette for a lot less money.*

Amazing. More for less. For 1978, we added eighteen new standard features to Chevette and still kept the price below last year's Chevette with the same equipment.
Some of the new standard features on the 1978 Chevy Chevette: 1. AM radio. 2. Whitewall tires. 3. 1.6 Litre engine. 4. Bumper rub strips. 5. Sport steering wheel. 6. Body side moldings. 7. Console. 8. Swing-out rear windows. 9. Wheel trim rings. 10. Cigarette lighter. 11. Color-keyed instrument panel. 12. Glove compartment lock. 13. Deluxe

grille. 14. Reclining bucket seats.** And more . . . 18 in all!
And you still get all this standard, too: 15. Four-foot-wide hatch. 16. Front disc brakes. 17. Delco Freedom battery. 18. Rack-and-pinion steering. 19. Carpeting. 20. Fold-down rear seat. 21. Short 30.2-foot turning circle. 22. Fully synchronized 4-Speed transmission. 23. Retractable seat belts. 24. Diagnostic connector. 25. Strong unitized body. 26. "Smart Switch". 27. Plus an extensive dealer organization from coast to coast. And more . . . .

All things considered, the new '78 Chevette is considerably more car. At a very considerable value.
*Comparison of manufacturer's suggested retail price for a 1977 Chevette Coupe with options now standard on 1978 Chevette Coupe.
**Some early production Chevettes in dealer inventory will not have reclining seats. The suggested base price will be reduced accordingly.

SEE WHAT'S NEW TODAY IN A CHEVROLET.

Motor: Standard

In an age of options, Chevy opted to show all of the Chevette's generous standard features. While other manufacturers pushed air-conditioning, sun roofs, and turbochargers, Chevette stuck to the basics.

Ford ad featured a woman exclaiming over Ford's featured glovebox, "I can put my purse and papers in it and know they're safe."

In the 1950s, Chevrolet's quest for the ultimate comfort mobile involved sending "20 million questionnaires to car owners, covering even such things as the preferred location for the ash tray." As drivers spent more time commuting and vacationing, cars became complete home entertainment systems with radios, eight-track stereos, dictation machines, small record players, and even televisions. TV, however, wasn't conducive

Sexy Steering Wheels

Although the "more" is only alluded to in the text, this 1964 ad pulls no punches by insinuating the loving potential of the "Tilt and Telescoping Steering Wheel." Make-out features in autos were not new, however. They stretched all the way back to 1925 with Jewett cars' fold-down bed. The prudish Henry Ford, on the other hand, wouldn't submit to such debauchery and supposedly made the bench in the Model T only 38 inches long to avoid his automobiles turning into portable love shacks according to James Fink in *Automobile Age*.

CADILLAC DOES MORE THAN TILT THE STEERING WHEEL

Cadillac's newest version of its famed Tilt Wheel permits you to move the steering wheel toward you or away from you. The unique Tilt and Telescoping Steering Wheel is available only with Cadillac, adjustable at a finger touch to the position that best suits your body build. The short driver enjoys an unobstructed, clear-ahead view of the road. The heavier driver can move the wheel up and away for more suitable spaciousness. The angle and height of the wheel can be adjusted for precise arm reach. Any driver can position and reposition the wheel, even while driving, for constant ease and comfort on long highway journeys. And the wheel can be swung up and away for easier entry and exit. Cadillac's Tilt and Telescoping Steering Wheel is like the individual tailoring of a fine custom garment. It permits you to fashion your Cadillac to your own distinctive dimensions for unparalleled driving pleasure. The Tilt and Telescoping Steering Wheel is a product of Saginaw Steering Gear Division, General Motors Corporation, Saginaw, Michigan.

to driving in traffic. A radio renaissance dawned in the 1950s with DJs like Wolfman Jack replacing the radio drama of the prewar era.

In the 1960s, options could cost half again as much as the car. The 1964 Ford Mustang sold for $2,368 with an average option package running $1,000, of which more than 400,000 sold in the first six months. The 1962 Ford Thunderbird SportsRoadster even offered an altimeter, as though it were ready to head into space.

While dubious options became the norm in the early 1960s, the safety craze led by Ralph Nader saw the introduction of seat belts as standard equipment on January 1, 1964. In 1966, the Motor Vehicle Safety Act set standards for seat belts, padded dashes and sun screens, dual brakes, bumper heights, control knobs on the dash that didn't stick out as far, and steering columns that would collapse upon impact. In the 1970s, further standards were set on bumpers and padded dashboards, roofs and moldings, and in the 1990s, airbags and automatic seat belts became a requirement.

Options that had become standard features had run the course from being special amenities for supposedly delicate women to practical safety features for delicate skulls. ■

27

*"This oil crisis is confusing the public.
People aren't buying the cars that are best for them."*
—General Motors executive

★ ★ ★

In 1907, the Mason Car Sales Company promised its buggy could travel "475 miles on 18 gallons gasoline," or 26 miles per gallon, making it the "best 2-cylinder car in America." Plymouth could sing the praises of its 24-mile-per-gallon touring sedan in 1937. Dodge could boast 22 miles per gallon the same year. The 1949 135-horsepower Packard made the estimated 19 miles per gallon of its Eight the center of its advertising campaign. Over the years, American car manufacturers traded fuel efficiency for size and power. As cars became more adept at "rocketing" down the highway, owners grew less assured that their gas-guzzlers would make it to the next roadside filling station. By 1974, EPA estimates like 7.9 miles per gallon for the Lincoln Continental or 7.6 miles per gallon for the Oldsmobile 98 Regency were predictably absent from ads.

In the decades following World War II, Americans consumed gas like a nicotine-starved smoker sucks Camels. The thriving postwar economy,

The efficiency of The New Chevrolet

**More efficient use of space than before.
More ease of maintenance than before.
More mileage than before. Because efficiency is important. And Chevrolet wants to bring you more.***

*All comparisons relate to the 1976 full-size Chevrolet.

Perhaps the last thing you'd expect in a six-passenger car is efficiency.
Comfort, room and quiet? Of course.
But efficiency?
Well, we think The New Chevrolet will change your perception about what to expect in six-passenger cars.
Because it is comfortable. It is roomy. It is quiet. But remarkably, it is also efficient.

More mileage.
A nifty little book published by the U.S. Government—the 1977 EPA Guide for New Car Buyers—reports that The New Chevrolet, equipped with automatic transmission, has mileage estimates of 22 mpg highway, 17 mpg city with its new standard Six; 21 mpg highway, 16 mpg city with its new available 305 cu. V8.
Both are noticeable improvements over last year's standard engine.
Remember though, your mileage may vary depending on how you drive, the condition of your car, and how it is equipped. Also, EPA estimates for California are lower.

More rear seat leg room and more head room.
While taking up less room in the world, The New Chevrolet actually manages to provide more leg room for your rear seat passengers, and more head room for everyone.
Not only that, but the added head room helps make it easier to get in and out of The New Chevrolet.

We know that quick, easy servicing is important to you. So we've given The New Chevrolet an engine diagnostic terminal that helps make 35 electrical checks, quickly and easily. Also, a Freedom battery that never needs water or scheduled maintenance.

Five more cubic feet.
Based on the U.S. Government estimates of interior vehicle size—as reported in the 1977 EPA Guide for New Car Buyer—that's how much more room The New Chevrolet has compared to the older style, full-size cars still being offered by our nearest sales competitor. And no one needs to tell you how important interior room is to your comfort.

The New Chevrolet has a shorter turning circle. Making it more manageable in tight spaces, more manageable in city traffic.

The Caprice Classic Sedan

More trunk room.
Thanks once again to its more efficient design, The New Chevrolet also gives you more trunk room. A whopping 20.2 cu. ft. in the Sedan.

Also, more enjoyment.
It's increasingly important for all cars to be more efficient. In their use of materials. In their use of natural resources. But that doesn't mean they should be dull. Or spartan. Or boring. And The New Chevrolet isn't. As your very first test drive will tell you.

• MORE INNOVATIONS.
• MORE HEAD ROOM.
• MORE REAR SEAT LEG ROOM.
• MORE TRUNK ROOM.
• MORE MILES TO THE GALLON.
• MORE CORROSION PROTECTION.
• MORE EASE OF ENTRY AND EXIT.
• MORE EASE OF MAINTENANCE.
• MORE VALUES FOR YOUR MONEY.

Now that's more like it.

New, improved, 16-mpg Chevy!
In the 1970s, the dominance of American "gas-guzzlers" was severely challenged by fuel-efficient foreign compacts. Domestic manufacturers desperately tried to convince buyers there were more important things than those miles-per-gallon figures. "Efficiency" for the 1977 Chevrolet meant better use of space, not gas mileage—plenty of room to stretch your legs while waiting in those long gas lines!

increased automobile ownership, and the development of American car culture were all fueled by a seemingly infinite supply of low-priced gasoline. This all ended in the 1970s as both the federal government and the person on the street realized the times were changing. In 1973, the Organization of Petroleum Exporting Countries (OPEC) protested American support of Israel in the Yom Kippur War by withholding its supply of oil. Gas prices quickly doubled and the resulting energy crisis forced motorists to sit in gas lines for hours on end. People committed armed robbery and even murder just to fill the tank of their Matador or Grand Prix.

Even before the oil embargo, many protested Detroit's infatuation with giant, gas-hungry automobiles. *Consumer Reports* claimed 1970 American consumers did not want "the overpowered and overpriced extensions of the childish imagination that Detroit would prefer to sell. They do not want to 'turn their driveways into launching pads!'" Foreign compacts flooded the U.S. market, and many consumers opted for these energy-conscious models. Washington took heed, and in 1975 passed the Energy Policy and Conservation Act. The act mandated that new cars meet the Corporate Average Fuel Economy (CAFE) of 18 miles per gallon by 1978 and 27.5 miles per gallon by 1985, thus forcing a reversal of American manufacturers' long tradition of trading efficiency for power. Dollars that used to go into styling innovations were now diverted to the engineering department.

The energy shortage and Federal safety and emission regulations left many drivers longing for the uncompromising cars of old, those in which demonstrating machismo was as easy as lead-footing the gas pedal. In a review of one new high-performance Italian sports car at this time, a reporter vented, "While you and I are lumping along in our sensible semicrashproof sedans, eyes scanning the speedometer, lest we exceed 55 miles per hour, and the gas gauge, fearful that our hungry engine will consume its last drop of fuel before the Arabs shut off the spigot, we can comfort (or torment,

"Econo-master engine!"
Fuel efficiency has been a selling point as long as folks have been hawking automobiles. The 1939 Olds Sixty promised its 90-horsepower engine would be easy on the pocketbook and allow the driver to whiz past the gas pumps.

depending on your frame of mind) ourselves with the thought that a few places still exist on this earth where automobiles are viewed as uncompromising, balls-to-the-wall-oh-my-God mechanisms of pure hedonism." Americans in the 1970s could only dream that someone somewhere was having fun in an automobile, and take heart that at least they were better off than victims in the disaster films that filled the nation's theaters. ∎

"Guests of Honor" Wherever They Go!

Not long after a motorist takes delivery of his first Cadillac car, he makes a truly wonderful and thrilling discovery.

No matter where he travels at the wheel of his Cadillac, he finds that he is accorded an *extra* measure of courtesy and respect.

And this discovery will be all the more rewarding for the man or woman who makes the move to Cadillac in 1955. For the "car of cars" now offers more of everything to inspire the respect and admiration of people everywhere.

Its world-famous beauty, for example, is more majestic and distinctive than ever before. Its celebrated interior luxury and elegance are far more wonderful to behold . . . and to enjoy. And its performance is, from every standpoint, the finest in Cadillac history!

If you haven't as yet inspected and driven the magnificent 1955 Cadillac—you ought to do so soon at your Cadillac dealer's.

You'll be a most welcome guest—at any time!

CADILLAC MOTOR CAR DIVISION ★ GENERAL MOTORS CORPORATION

SELLING STATUS

"What does your car say about you?"
—1964 Lincoln ad

"Bloodlines count . . . in cars as well as horses," declared Mrs. Priscilla St. George Duke in a 1941 ad for Studebaker, clarifying once and for all that in the age of automobility

transportation still symbolized social standing. Before the days of the auto, city people's wealth or standing could be calculated by the distance between their bedroom and

It's a Bird! It's a Plane! It's a Graham!
"So eager, so alive, so restless . . . it looks like it's going when it's standing still!" boasts the ad copy from this 1938 Graham. The "Graham is safest car in America today" with headlights aerodynamically built into the fenders—just like the postwar Tucker, which also had a moving center light that turned with the wheels. For just a slightly higher fee, you too could have this "Rich Man's Luxury." *Steve Hanson Collection*

1955 Coup de Ville
Cadillac aristocrats were met by doormen wherever they went, as demonstrated in this ad. The car "offers more of everything to inspire the respect and admiration of people everywhere."

their smelly horse stable. The middling sorts had no choice but to keep their horses on their own property, allowing the fumes to waft through their homes and penetrate the bedclothes. Those of more substantial means could afford to "park" their team across town under somebody else's window and avoid showing up at high-society parties smelling like spent oats.

By the early 1920s the system had completely reversed. Affluent homes started featuring garages with the understanding that car owners never wanted to be too far from their new mechanical family members. Driveways and integrated garages were quick to follow. By the time of the postwar ranch house, many garages took up one third of a dwelling's floor space. Suburbanites had to decide if it was more impressive to park their car under cover of the twin garage or leave it in the driveway for all to see. Maybe it depended on whether the car was a new Caddy or a tired old Hudson.

Advertising has often tried to link automobiles with status and social standing. Copywriters developed a sophisticated way of talking about status in the early years of car advertising that is still in use today. It goes far beyond the simple formula of wearing one's bank account on one's wheels. Pitching different ideas of status to audiences of varying means, they told the rich to flaunt it shamelessly and the middle class that there were things more important than fancy cars. Ads claimed that status could be had by driving the same car as the stars or driving a little piece of old Europe. Some preached the merits of hopping on the bandwagon, while others touted the value of standing apart from the crowd. Still others, as demonstrated by the 1938 ad for Graham, claimed that looks could be pleasantly deceiving—one could look rich without dropping too many oats. ■

A BREED APART: THE CADILLAC ARISTOCRAT

"Nothing has spread socialistic feeling in this country more than the use of the automobile. To the country man, they are a picture of the arrogance of wealth, with all its independence and carelessness."
—Woodrow Wilson, 1906

★ ★ ★

Tuxedos, furs, and jewels, jewels, jewels! Early automobile ads went to great lengths to portray their products as fashion accessories of the ultra rich. The "favored few" were repeatedly pictured attending parties at luxurious mansions, setting out on expensive yachts or airplanes, and

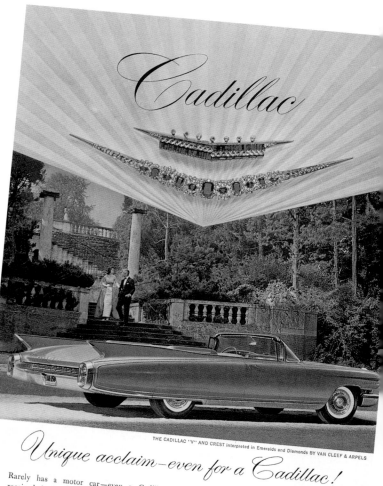

THE CADILLAC "V" AND CREST interpreted in Emeralds and Diamonds BY VAN CLEEF & ARPELS

Unique acclaim—even for a Cadillac!

Rarely has a motor car—even a Cadillac—received the high degree of public acclaim that has attended the introduction of the 1960 "car of cars". This praise has, indeed, been heart-warming. But it has also, we feel, been entirely logical. Certainly, no one could question the fact of its great beauty and luxury—so inspiring that it has already established a new era of automotive elegance. And surely, no one could deny the brilliance of its new performance—smooth, quiet, silken and eager beyond any previous Cadillac standard. Have you seen and driven the 1960 Cadillac for yourself? If not, you should do so at your earliest opportunity. We feel certain that you will give it your unqualified endorsement. CADILLAC MOTOR CAR DIVISION · GENERAL MOTORS CORPORATION

A Jewel of a Car
This 1960 ad was one in a long series featuring designer jewels. The association with such handcrafted luxury items declared the Cadillac was a breed apart from other mass-produced automobiles.

illustrating the ever-popular theme of waiting for a servant to open one's car door. "What does your car say about you?" asked one series of ads. The luxury car proclaimed the size of one's bank account. According to many ads, it also declared the owner's superiority over those who did not drive such flashy wheels.

No American car pushed this concept as far nor as long as the Cadillac. For years, ad copy claimed the Cadillac owner was a breed apart from the average motorist. "No matter where he travels at the wheel of his Cadillac, he finds that he is accorded an *extra* measure of courtesy and respect." "Wherever you go you will find these distinguished cars the pronounced favorites in the smartest and most exclusive circles."

Several advertising techniques were used to create an exclusive image for the Cadillac aristocrat. Many ads suggested the auto was created by artisans rather than produced on an assembly line—"a masterpiece from the master craftsmen." The ads evoked images of a preindustrial past in which products were valued for their rarity and handmade qualities. Custom gowns, furs, and jewelry appeared in several series of Cadillac ads, and their designers were credited by name: "Gowns by Irene," "Jewels by Cartier." In the early 1960s, the carmaker introduced its "mink test." Women decked out in their second skins would sit down in the car, fidget around, then check whether the seat coverings had messed up their furs. An important concern for any car owner!

Everybody served the Cadillac aristocrats. They always wore formal evening wear and were waited on at five-star restaurants. Doormen greeted them wherever they went, invariably admiring the automobile out of the corner of their eye. When human attendants were absent, the Cadillac itself was a pliant servant. "The car will be at your service." The "eagerly responsive" car "is waiting for you." The Cadillac owner "finds it reassuring to know that the car is capable of such extraordinary service." The cars did not even ask for Thursdays and every other Sunday off.

The exclusive world of the Cadillac aristocrat harked back to advertising images from the first decades of automobile production. Before the introduction of Ford's Model N and Model T, car owners were found in the select set of those that could afford the expensive toys. Wealthy sportsmen, doctors, and businessmen were the first to

Caddie Cosmetics
The 1929 Cadillac-La Salle was presented as a fashion accessory of the ultra-rich.

putt through dung-piled city streets in their iron horses. Ownership of any car was a mark of affluence, and most manufacturers stressed this point in their advertisements. Woodrow Wilson echoed this in his 1906 pronouncement that the automobile would lead to socialism by fostering envy of the rich. Automobile ownership quickly expanded to include other income brackets, but it was not until after World War II that ownership became widely available to the working class and lost much of its air of exclusivity. Advertisements for other models were aimed at the new mass market, but the luxury car endured for those who wanted to set themselves apart from the crowd. For decades, the Cadillac remained the quintessential way for "old money" and the *nouveau riche* to declare themselves a breed apart. ■

The most famous Cadillac aristocrat was the "Fisher Body Girl." For years following her creation in the late 1920s, she was the center of advertisements for the Fisher Body Division of General Motors. She appeared in scores of ads and occasionally surfaced in cleverly devised cameos in the feature pages of national magazines. Such continuous exposure made her one of the most recognized corporate mascots of the time and established a level of name recognition for Fisher that surpassed those of some full-fledged auto manufacturers.

The "Fisher Body Girl" helped define the look of the stylish modern woman. Always dressed to the nines, she lived in a world of mansions, opera, gentlemanly sports, and shopping. She was always on the go and trying new things, yet she often maintained an almost passive expression somewhere between mild lack of interest and complete boredom. Women readers, advertisers maintained, strongly identified with the "Fisher Body Girl" and her impeccable fashion sense.

Automobiles rarely appeared in the early advertisements featuring the "Fisher Body Girl." Her body took the place of the auto body in the ads, and Fisher's slogan "Look to the body!" was one of the least-veiled sexual innuendoes in auto ads of the period. In fact, the character's body was portrayed as everything Fisher wanted in the auto bodies it manufactured. She was a slave to fashion, able to change her look much more regularly than the company could retool their machines. She was also long and slender, often unnaturally so. McClelland Barclay, the creator and illustrator of the "Fisher Body Girl," frequently distorted her proportions, exaggerating the span of her body, legs, and arms much as later illustrators would stretch Cadillacs to the length of Route 66. Once photographs replaced illustrations of the "Fisher Body Girl" in the late 1930s, it became apparent that she was not really that tall and skinny—she was just drawn that way. ■

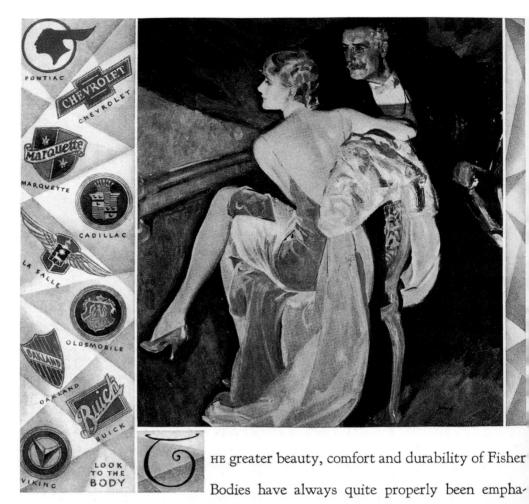

ΤHE greater beauty, comfort and durability of Fisher Bodies have always quite properly been emphasized, but the really vital thing about them — today more than ever in the past — is that they give a car greater value. That value extends throughout every Fisher Body and reveals itself convincingly in greater beauty, comfort, durability and strength. General Motors cars — and those cars only — bring to the motor car buyer the benefits of Body by Fisher. This joining of a higher value body with a higher value chassis completes a car of so much greater value, that to most buyers it will seem obviously futile to seek its equal anywhere but in a higher price field.

GENERAL MOTORS

PROUD TO BE A FACE IN THE CROWD

"I will build a motor car for the great multitude."
—1909 Ford ad

★ ★ ★

In 1930, José Ortega y Gasset wrote *The Revolt of the Masses*, his polemic against the "common man," who no longer appreciated his own inferiority but demanded a central role in 20th-century society and culture. "The mass has decided to advance to the foreground of social life, to occupy the places, to use the instruments and to enjoy the pleasures hitherto reserved to the few."

Join the Many Thousands Switching to Plymouth!

❶ See the 1940 Quality Chart. It clearly compares "All 3" low-priced cars for size, safety, luxury, and fine engineering.
❷ Take Plymouth's delightful Luxury Ride to complete the evidence that Plymouth gives you more car for your money.

THE 1940 QUALITY CHART
Comparison of "All Three" Low-Priced Cars with Leading High-Priced Cars in One

YOU CAN PICK THE BIGGEST VALUE THIS EASY "ONE-TWO" WAY

1. SEE THE QUALITY CHART FOR FACTS
2. TAKE THE LUXURY RIDE FOR PROOF

OF 22 QUALITY FEATURES FOUND IN HIGH-PRICED CARS—
Plymouth has 21. Car 2 has 11. Car 3 has 8

THOUSANDS of new owners are glad they switched to Plymouth . . . and you, too, can benefit from the "One-Two" buying method.

Plymouth is the only one of "All 3" *low-priced* cars that gives you a majority of the 22 important quality features

found in high-priced cars.

See the 1940 Quality Chart at your Plymouth dealer's. Then take Plymouth's Luxury Ride. Plymouth is easy to buy! PLYMOUTH DIVISION OF CHRYSLER CORPORATION.

TUNE IN MAJOR BOWES' HOUR, C.B.S., THURS., 9 TO 10 P.M., E.S.T.
BUSINESS MEN: See the new low-priced Plymouth Commercial Cars.

1940 PLYMOUTH COUPES $645 START AT | SEDANS $699 START AT
—Delivered in Detroit, Mich. Prices include Federal taxes. Transportation and state, local taxes, if any, not included.
PLYMOUTH BUILDS GREAT CARS

Thousands of Owners Cannot Be Wrong
Mass popularity was a virtue of the 1940 Plymouth. The frantic tabloid layout was typical of appeals to "mass" audiences. Similarly, the scientific quest for "facts" and "proof," ever aided by the scientific expert, was often cited as the basis of informed consumerism.

ESSEX
THE CHALLENGER

A Wide Choice of Colors at No Extra Cost

Hosts of other Car Owners
Join the Big Swing to ESSEX

ESSEX the Challenger sweeps aside the barriers of price class. It challenges the performance, the style, the luxurious, roomy comfort of any car at any price, on the basis that no other car gives you back so much for every dollar you put in.

That is why the acceptance of Essex the Challenger is the talk of motordom. Join the van of 1,000,000 Super-Six owners who are demonstrating its right and ability to challenge the best that motordom offers.

$695
AND UP - AT FACTORY

Standard Equipment includes: *4 hydraulic shock absorbers—electric gauge for gas and oil—radiator shutters—saddle lamps—windshield wiper—glareproof rear view mirror—electrolock—controls on steering wheel—all bright parts chromium-plated.*

Conformity as Sales Pitch
The 1925 Essex boasted not a bandwagon but a "van of 1,000,000 Super-Six owners." As cars became less expensive, advertisers courted a mass of like-minded consumers who wanted to be "just like everybody else."

Willys-Knight agreed. In 1928, the company declared a "triumph of American industry: Rich man's car brought within reach of general public by magic of quantity production." This democratization of the auto got under Ortega's skin. He believed the "barbaric" masses did not appreciate their good fortune. Like an angry father whose spoiled children did not acknowledge his sacrifices, Ortega wailed, "The world is a civilized one; its inhabitant is not: he does not see the civilization of the world around him, but he uses it as if it were a natural force. The new man wants his motor-car, and enjoys it, but he believes that it is the spontaneous fruit of an Edenic tree."

The Revolt of the Masses found favor among many advertising leaders. It suggested that they were superior to their audience. It echoed popular mass psychological studies that claimed "the average intelligence of the American people is that of a 13-year-old child." Yet perhaps more influential on the advertising industry was Ortega's contention that the majority of people did not try to distinguish themselves but took pride in being "just like everybody else."

The 1920s and 1930s witnessed a spate of advertisements that encouraged people to purchase a car because everyone else was buying it. Unlike ads for Cadillac and other luxury cars that stressed the importance of standing apart from the crowd, these ads assumed jumping on the bandwagon was a universal goal. The race was on to create the image of a true *Volkswagen* or "people's car." Mass production of identical products and a mass media of identical opinions created a mass market of identical consumers. Or so the logic went. If there did exist a mass of like-minded consumers, shouldn't they all buy the same automobile? The problem, of course, was that no common *volk* existed in America, if anywhere. Class, ethnicity, and style separated the American "mass" into a number of different buying publics, and the auto's early role as a status symbol persisted as car-owners continued to use their automobiles to set themselves apart from those around them. ■

Envy as Sales Pitch
Once the masses jumped on the automobile-buying bandwagon they settled in for the ride and took stock of the other passengers. This 1937 Packard pitch shows what advertisers expected they were thinking. *Steve Hanson Collection*

HERE WE ARE....*ENVYING*

Did we envy the Dexters in their new Packard? The honest answer is…*yes!* Emphatically, *yes!* We had always wanted a Packard. We felt we'd almost give our good right arms to be sitting there like the Dexters, heads in the clouds, with people saying "Hmm, they sure must be making good."…Then

we got to thinking—I made as much as Ed Dexter. If he could afford a Packard, why couldn't I? Well, why *couldn't* I?…So we marched down to the Packard showroom to look at the new Packard 120 and the new Packard Six, and to ask a lot of questions…

HERE WE ARE....*BEING ENVIED*

And as a result, we're no longer on the outside, envying. We're on the *inside* being envied. On the inside of our new Packard. We found out that our old car took full care of down payment, and that this new Packard was ours for only $35 *a month!* We've found out it costs no more to service than the small car we

used to own. You can't imagine the kick we're getting out of owning and driving a Packard. We're as thrilled as a couple of kids. And we're telling our friends to get wise…to learn how easy it is now to *be* the man who owns one!

★   ASK THE MAN WHO OWNS ONE   ★

DOWN WITH THE JONESES

"More people named Jones own Chevrolets than any other car!"
—*1956 Chevrolet ad*

★ ★ ★

Depending on one's point of view, the "democracy of goods" afforded by American mass production resulted in either a bland, predictable sameness or a beautiful classless society. Pete Seeger complained about little boxes that all looked just the same, yet Andy Warhol cheered, "What's great about this country is that America started the tradition where the richest consumers buy essentially the same things as the poorest. A Coke is a Coke and no amount of money can get you a better Coke than the one the bum on the corner is drinking. All the Cokes are the same and all the Cokes are good. Liz Taylor knows it, the President knows it, the bum knows it, and you know it." Automobiles were not as similar as soft drinks. In a consumer culture awash in mass-produced goods, some ads suggested that not all American Dreams were created equal.

New automobiles were the perfect way to breed the envy of the neighborhood. One could drive a 1959 Thunderbird, "the car everyone would love to own," or be assured that "they'll know you arrived when you drive up in an Edsel." Such ads played to consumers' sense of individualism and status. They also acknowledged the desire to conform. Market researchers found that many people wanted to impress, but feared a new car that was too flashy might cause neighbors to consider them snobbish. "The job, then, is not to keep up with the Joneses. It's to keep *down* with them," declared William H. Whyte, former editor of *Fortune* magazine in 1956. The perfect car was showy and exciting enough to induce envy yet so practical and conservative that the owner would still get invited to neighborhood parties. The Cadillac ad established its owner as a wealthy aristocrat. These ads placed their car owners out front in terms of fashion. When the masses were yearning to hop on, they said that you could be *driving* the bandwagon. ■

"My, the neighbors sure like our New '52 Dodge!"

Let the "Show Down" Way show you why Dodge is so popular

This smart, new Dodge wins admirers with its looks . . . wins hearts with its dependable day-in, day-out performance. You get modern styling—advanced engineering that protects your investment for years ahead. Among its many exciting features is the amazing Dodge Oriflow Ride that makes every mile you travel boulevard-smooth. And if you think this is just sales talk—your Dodge dealer can give you *proof!* Before you buy a car in *any* price class, ask him for a free copy of the "Show Down" Plan. It lets you compare Dodge feature by feature against other cars for greater driving ease, comfort and safety . . . greater value. Once you've made this comparison test, we're sure you'll see why "You could pay hundreds of dollars more and still not get all Dodge gives you!"

Specifications and Equipment Subject to Change Without Notice

Big, new, dependable '52 **DODGE**

CORONET SIERRA
4-Door Station Wagon

Dick and Jane Jones
The shiny, red Coronet Sierra was just the car to get the neighbors' motors running. It was practical and dependable enough to be called a necessity, yet the white-walls, chrome, and "Oriflow Ride" set the owners apart from the average Dick and Jane.

FEELING RICH

*"'There is a very costly car' you would say
if you did not know the price."*
—1929 Hudson ad

★　★　★

Autos that could not compete with the luxury of the Cadillac or Lincoln Continental claimed in their ads that the right car could make up in style what its driver lacked in riches. Several automobile advertisements touted the value and dignity of owning mid-priced cars. Some criticized the industry's tendency to equate expensive cars with high status. "One of our people has a psychologist friend and the friend says that the auto is bought as a status symbol in many cases, as a reflection of the owner's position, importance and take home pay. Well, now maybe that's the reason a lot of people buy higher priced cars instead of Chevrolets. . . . Because it couldn't really be a matter of more room, say . . . or power . . . or ride and roadability," reasoned one ad. Copy confronted those who said money brings happiness. The 1969 Chevy Caprice "almost takes the fun out of being rich." Members of a 1958 suburban family could stand by their Plymouth and declare, "We're not the richest people in town . . . but we're the proudest!"

During the recession and oil crises of the 1970s, several ads tried to make thrift fashionable. Some ads for mid- and low-priced automobiles courted those who could afford a more expensive model. Car buyers were told, "Live below your means." Chevrolet loved "those who don't buy the most expensive car they can." This technique was mastered in advertisements for small foreign compacts. One 1972 ad summed it up: when your neighbor goes to Acapulco, "you go to the zoo and a Mexican restaurant. He gets that Chevy, you go for the Honda Coupe." These ads told the wealthy consumer it was stylish to drive an inexpensive car. They also assured the buyer who was not rich that his car was the only thing small about him. American manufacturers found it difficult to compete in this game of "onedownsmanship." The large bodies and big engines that for decades had been major attractions of American autos were now liabilities. Sales of American cars fell accordingly. In 1974, United States manufacturers sold 23 percent fewer cars than they had the previous year. ■

Squint slightly. Now couldn't this Caprice almost pass for a you-know-what?

Cars Make You Richer
Furs? Evening wear? A doorman? Must be a Cadillac aristocrat! But wait! The 1967 Caprice duplicates that fancy feeling so well that even Caddy owners are moving down to this designer impostor. Those that cannot afford a Cadillac are assured in another ad from the series that the Caprice "can make you feel richer." That's enough for me!

Rich and Poor
Some ads played up the relationship between price and status. This 1923 ad, however, suggested both the rich and those of "more limited means" could enjoy Chevrolet style.

Millionaire Mobile

"If I'd been a millionaire I couldn't have given them more pleasure!" A 1958 lesson in selling mid-priced cars to middle-income consumers. Upwardly mobile families placed as much pride in striving for their American Dream as in achieving it.

New Rambler Country Club Hardtop model, styled by Pinin Farina. Hood ornament designed by Petty, white sidewall tires are optional.

Announcing Another Pinin Farina Masterpiece

The New 1953 Rambler

Now the Popular Nash Rambler sparkles with the last word in continental styling! In every elegant detail you'll see the glamour, the custom luxury, the *genius* that Pinin Farina—and only Farina—can lavish on a car. Yes, you will see it all in the first car designed for today's traffic!

New Style—New Vision!
Now the new windshield is "picture-window" wide and deeper, with 25% more glass. Now there's a rakish new slope to the hood, a new functional air-scoop . . . new "Road-Guide" fenders . . . a sweeping, new flair to the racy rear . . . a swanky new continental rear tire mount.

Dual-Range Hydra-Matic!
Now there's added power in the Super Flying Scot engine—yet you'll still get record-breaking Rambler gasoline economy. And, with new Dual-Range Hydra-Matic Drive, you can *Ramble* all day without shifting!

True to Nash Rambler tradition, this most luxurious of compact cars gives you custom accessories like radio, Weather Eye Conditioned Air System —even the continental rear tire mount—*included* in the standard price.

On Display Now!
You still haven't heard *half* the Nash Rambler news! Come in and see America's newest—the Nash Rambler "Country Club", the Station Wagon, the Convertible Sedan.

For 1953 There's None So New As

Airflytes
The Ambassador • The Statesman • The Rambler
Great Cars Since 1902
Nash Motors, Div. Nash-Kelvinator Corporation, Detroit, Mich.

"Beep Beep" Goes the "Little Nash Rambler"

So went the 1950s song making the Rambler famous as it zooms, in only second gear, past a Cadillac. Nash hired the Italian designer Pinin Farina, who had styled Ferraris, to add some continental flair to the model, hoping to squelch the company's reputation of having bathtub-inspired bodies. Nevertheless, the Rambler isn't *nearly* as long as this painting suggests (keep in mind that the 1950 Nash Rambler was supposedly the first "compact" American car). Nash's ads didn't dwell on the European look-alike theme, with fancy foreign words like Chevrolet's 1955 Motoramic ad, "Mesdemoiselles go for Chevrolet—everywhere they go *(and vice versa)*." Farina's savoir faire couldn't save Nash. The next year it merged with Hudson to form American Motors Corporation (AMC), making this 1953 Rambler one of the last Nashes. P.S. The "flying lady" hood ornament cost extra.

"The only car that could, or can, make a Paris frock happy!"
—1929 Hupmobile

★   ★   ★

1925 Wills Sainte Claire
While most makes skirted the subject of their co-opting European themes in their names, designs, and engines, Wills could only compare itself to all the best European qualities. Meanwhile, Ford's Lincoln declared itself one of the "Salon Favorites."

Even though the proliferation of cars was mostly an American phenomenon (although Paris often boasted more cars than New York), auto advertisers harped on the Continental qualities of their wares. Models' names were often European, such as Monaco, Toronado, Volare, Le Mans, and Grand Prix. "Powered Like Europe's Finest!" was the Willys-Knight ad of 1924. Willys compared its engine to the Daimler, Panhard, Mercedes-Benz, and Minerva of England, France, Germany, and Belgium, respectively. The emblem of the LaFayette Motors Corporation of Milwaukee, Wisconsin, combined American patriotism with old-world pomp and circumstance. It featured a pseudo bas-relief of the famous French General LaFayette who helped blast the British out of the United States. Cadillac pictured its 1927 La Salle in front of a quaint village in Normandy with the chic, mobilized Americans asking the rustic native, "*Comprenez-vous?*" Who says Europeans are one up on Americans? This series of ads featured Americans throughout France with glib titles like, "*La beauté et l'utilité*," "*La nouvelle arrivée*," and "*À la campagne.*" It wasn't until later that other makes would offer the name Parisienne and Continental to lure the Euro jet set. The Lincoln Continental was introduced in 1939 as a response to the 1938 Y-Job "dream car" shown by GM. A young Edsel Ford is said to have thought up this curvaceous car without styling gimmicks. And although the elder Ford wanted nothing to do with it, in 1941 the Museum of Modern Art named it a masterpiece of product design.

The new American car with the European look!

It's the breath-taking new 1953 Studebaker! Excitingly new in continental styling! Impressively down to earth in price!

THE dramatic 1953 Studebaker comes to you straight out of the dream book.
It sparkles with the verve and flair of Europe's most distinguished cars—and it's a thoroughly American car in comfort and handling ease.
It's completely, spectacularly new inside and outside. Sedans, coupes and hard-tops all gleam with enormous new

areas of glass for full vision.
You get all this marvelous new distinction at a down-to-earth price—with Studebaker low operating cost!
Order your '53 Studebaker now—a Champion in the lowest price field—a brilliant-performing Commander V-8.
Motoring's finest new Power Steering is available in Commanders at moderate extra cost.

New 1953 Studebaker

It's a startler! It's a Starliner!
The new Studebaker hardtop! Less than five feet high!
Truly a new flight into the future!

"It's a startler! It's a Starliner!"
Studebaker caught the wave with this dashing 1953 Starliner, powered by a Commander V-8. "With real foreign-car distinction" the Parisian wannabe Starliner (from Old World South Bend, Indiana) is headed for a plunge in the Seine or at least a parking ticket from a grimacing *gendarme*. The ad claims this is an "actual color photograph" illustrating "the verve and flair of expensive-looking foreign cars."

GIs returning from Europe after World War II carried stories of the perky British sports cars they had seen zipping around the English countryside. American car manufacturers were slow on the uptake, but when Chevy finally caught up, it created a masterpiece: the Corvette. In 1953, the 'Vette got mixed reviews. British sports-car enthusiasts pooh-poohed it as handling like a sick yak—probably because of the automatic transmission, which was unthinkable to European car enthusiasts. But the Corvette survived the killjoys and withstood the competition, even that offered by Ford's original two-seat Thunderbird.

European governments, on the other hand, were hesitant to recognize cars as a tool for the masses the way Henry Ford did, and continued to tax them as luxury items. With slow-growing domestic markets and a need for a postwar cash infusion, European manufacturers turned their attention to car-hungry America. The sports-car craze helped open the door for the first full-blown assault on the American marketplace by European manufacturers. And by 1958 they controlled more than 8 percent of the U.S. market. Their high-quality engines and sleek and slim designs caught the high-end market, while the Big Three just kept enlarging their mobiles with more chrome and vinyl frosting on top. ∎

"*DARNED CLEVER, those movie stars! Romantic, yes—
but practical too. That's why so many drive DeSoto!*"
—*1937 DeSoto ad*

★   ★   ★

Cars have been associated with the silver screen ever since the first horseless carriage. Hollywood adored the auto and filmed its history, from Bonnie and Clyde hot-wiring Ford V-8s to Tucker making his avant-garde automotive spaceships. Western roundups with cowboys and Indians shooting and spearing each other were replaced with modern vigilantes blasting the bad guys in endless car chases. A new genre was born.

Prior to the big screen, the car, like many stars, made its debut on Broadway in *The Great Automobile Mystery* between 1900 and 1910. With the postradio era came the first car-company-sponsored television show in 1949 for Buick, *Olsen & Johnson's Fireball Fun-for-All*. Soon, every car manufacturer had to have its name on the boob tube with the likes of the *Dinah Shore Chevy Show* and Danny Kaye's show in "living color," which featured Pat Boone and Carolyn Jones stumping for GM. Often the actual skits would meld right into the ads, making it impossible to change the channel for commercial breaks. Since sponsors usually only had a couple of ads to run, each show would run the same commercial a number of times.

For added public exposure and extra pocket change, TV and movie stars often participated in car advertising and promotions. Ed Sullivan was sponsored by Mercury, Bob Hope by Chrysler, and Studebaker sponsored the *Mr. Ed Show*—as long as their car could appear in many scenes. Ford even nabbed one of the greatest composers of the 20th century to pitch its cars: Leonard Bernstein.

As much as cars influenced Hollywood, its celebrities, in turn, affected Detroit. The breast-shaped bumper guards on the 1954 Caddie were nicknamed "Dagmars," after a similarly endowed actress. Harley Earl's use of aircraft motifs in the design of various GM cars was said to have been inspired in part by Charles Lindbergh's transatlantic flight. And even the success of *Star Wars* inspired advertisers to once again show their cars zooming through space like the Oldsmobile Futuramic ads of yore.

Charlie Chan at Monte Carlo
Warner Oland got free publicity for his movie, and the 1937 DeSoto got a celebrity endorsement. Before product placement was considered a fine art of subtle hints, advertisers pulled no punches in bringing their message home. I'll bet ol' Charlie Chan even got a free DeSoto out of this deal!
Steve Hanson Collection

The 1970s featured a dynamite line-up of stars with the likes of Farrah Fawcett begging the world to buy Mercury Cougars, Catherine Denueve pushing the Mercury Monarch, and of course Ricardo Montalban extolling the virtues of Chrysler's rich "Corinthian" leather.

All was not peachy in Tinseltown, however, as celebrity car accidents made headlines alongside endorsements. Jayne Mansfield lost her head in her Buick Electra 225, Hank Williams, Sr., died in his 1952 pink Cadillac, Ted Kennedy had some steering problems in his 1967 Oldsmobile 88 at Chappaquiddick, and of course, JFK had his final car ride in a 1961 convertible Lincoln. ■

Gone with the Dodge

When Clark Gable, one of the premier playboys of his time, endorsed this 1937 Dodge, it meant that any true gentleman had to have one and, of course, a pencil-thin mustache. The 1940 Dodge would later be heralded by daredevil Jimmie Lynch and his Death Dodgers as "A Red Blooded Car if there ever was one. Only Dodge could take the beating I give a car every day. Dodge has saved my life literally hundreds of times! I'd be a sucker to use any other car." Steve *Hanson Collection*

HERE'S THE NEW 1951 CAR

New Inside...New Outside
with a Completely New Kind of Ride

NOW THE SECRET'S OUT! In previews of this new car men and women in all walks of life were thrilled by a completely new riding principle, new styling and host of engineering improvements . . . amazed that any car offering so much, could cost so little.

TED WILLIAMS—"*When I first saw this new 1951 car, its smart look, its new engineering advances made me put it in the expensive car class!*" says baseball's great left-handed slugger.

BETTY HUTTON—"*It's so big, so roomy, with greater visibility for every passenger.*" (Soon to be seen in Cecil B. DeMille's "THE GREATEST SHOW ON EARTH"—a Paramount Release in Technicolor.)

Now on Display
New 1951

DODGE

DODGE VALUE DEPENDABILITY

FLOATS DOWN ROADS THAT STOP OTHER CARS
New Oriflow shock absorber system—a revolutionary advance in riding smoothness and comfort. City road or country road, cobblestones or corduroy—wheels *stay on the ground* —no wheel hop or bounce.

NEW IN MORE WAYS THAN CARS COSTING UP TO $1,000 MORE!

New Kind of Ride! New Oriflow shock absorber system based on an entirely new principle brings you a truly *new kind of ride*—over the same roads that jarred and "hammered" you in the past.

New "Watchtower" Visibility through the new wider windshield and deeper, wider rear window—for greater safety, comfort. Here's new spaciousness *inside* to let you ride relaxed, uncrowded. Yet, *outside*, its new beauty is sleek and trim for easier handling and parking.

Drive Without Shifting! Dodge GYRO-MATIC brings you America's lowest-priced automatic transmission to free you from gear-shifting— with *complete control* of your car under all driving conditions.

Dodge on Display
Ted Williams and Betty Hutton tell the world that their favorite car is a 1951 Dodge. Betty Hutton's testimonial even says, "Soon to be seen on Cecil B. DeMille's 'THE GREATEST SHOW ON EARTH.' " We might ask who, Hutton or the Dodge?

Here's Why Clark Gable Switched to Dodge

CLARK GABLE, famed screen star, now appearing in Metro-Goldwyn-Mayer's "Parnell," says: "I switched to Dodge because it handles so magnificently...it's astonishingly economical...and has all the swift smoothness I enjoy in driving."

Thank you, Mr. Gable! You're one of the thousands of motorists the country over—people who, like yourself, can afford the most expensive cars—who are switching to Dodge!

See this new Dodge! Drive it! And remember, Dodge now delivers for just a few dollars more than the lowest-priced cars!

Division of Chrysler Corporation

DODGE
Easy terms gladly arranged to fit your budget at low cost through Commercial Credit Company.

Imprint of Cadillac Power !

Deep in German mud, this M-24 has left its imprint of Cadillac power. For, like more than 10,000 tanks that have gone before it, the M-24 is powered by two Cadillac V-type engines, driving through two Cadillac Hydra-Matic transmissions.

It is no longer a secret that tanks built and powered by Cadillac have long been laying tracks to Victory in every battle sector of the globe. For, with the help of Army

Ordnance Engineers, we started building tanks for Army use more than 3 years ago. We have been steadily at it ever since.

The success of the Cadillac V-type engine and Hydra-Matic transmission in powering tanks —the ease with which these power units were adapted to tank use—and their inherent ability to bring a new degree of maneuverability to tank warfare—are all conclusive evidence of their fundamental soundness of design.

Abnormal wartime use has subjected both engine and transmission to tests never encountered in civilian service. As a result, they have been improved in many ways.

Every Sunday Afternoon . . . GENERAL MOTORS SYMPHONY OF THE AIR—NBC Network

CADILLAC MOTOR CAR DIVISION   GENERAL MOTORS CORPORATION

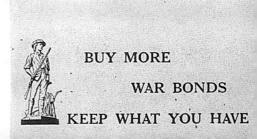

BUY MORE

WAR BONDS

KEEP WHAT YOU HAVE

WAR!!!

After Pearl Harbor and until the end of World War II, the U.S. auto industry shut down civilian production and put all of its efforts behind the making of war materiel. With no new vehicles to sell on the home front, advertising messages were shifted to support the war effort.

Some ads took on the harsh military power of their wares, like a Buick ad that read, "Life, Liberators and pursuit of the Axis. . . . Take a gang of young Americans . . . brief a target for them someplace where the Japs are thick, or where enemy factories cluster, ripe for the fall of a big stick of bombs." Or a Hudson ad showing their weaponry saving the day: "Scratch one Nazi pigboat!"

Other former car manufacturers like Nash chose to recount stories of individual people in the war and their hardships around it. One ad featured a man floating on a raft in the middle of the ocean thinking, "Sure, there'll be a

Cadillac Power!
Although far from the luxury of prewar Caddies or their postwar fins, GM tried to show the premier luxury car as an example of how GM could easily transfer its tool and die capabilities to powerful machines of any kind.

Uncle Sam's Jeep
Willys-Overland and Ford both made "jeeps"—short for GPV, which stood for General Purpose Vehicle. The jeep was the single most successful vehicle of World War II, causing it to see postwar domestic life as the first Sport Utility Vehicle. Wartime ads proclaimed, "Vive Les Americains! Vive La France! Vive Le Jeep!" One could also follow the advancement of the war through Willys' ads as, "Avenging jeeps blast Japs from Chinese Village!" And of course the postwar market was always a concern as Willys asked, "Will the 'Jeep' speed up farming?"

"And when that great day finally comes—when the last Nazi swastika is shot out of the sky—then you will find that from the crucible of war we have brought new skill into building the automobiles and refrigerators for America at peace."
—*1942 Nash Kelvinator ad*

parade. . . ." Others featured separated lovers wishing, "When you come back to me. . . ." as the man is in a Japanese POW camp surrounded by barbed wire saying, "Reading between the lines of your blessed letter . . ." Of course, all of this wasn't entirely altruistic. Nash, like other manufacturers, hoped that people would remember to shop its make of car when the war was finally over. ∎

TOUGH as nails. Fast as lightning. Dependable as the fighting men who man them—Willys-built Jeeps are sparking the attack of American and Allied fighting forces in every thundering theatre of war.

Willys-Overland engineers assisted the U. S. Quartermaster Corps in designing the Jeep—the motorized vehicle that has so effectively met the demands of mechanized warfare. The experienced hands of men who built thousands

"For accomplishing more than seemed reasonable or possible a year ago."
Under Secretary of War
ROBERT PATTERSON

of Willys Americars *for the people,* have to their credit the Willys-designed "Go-Devil" engine that drives all Jeeps built for the U. S. Army and our Allies.

This same type "Go-Devil" engine is in thousands of Willys Americars that are aiding the war effort on the home front. No other motor cars are getting war workers to their vital jobs with so great a saving in rubber, gasoline, and oil. Willys-Overland Motors, Inc.

The sun never sets on the fighting Jeep

WILLYS

THE WAR OF THE FACTORIES

Full-scale mass production of cars began in the United States, and before World War II, the Axis tried desperately to keep up. Britain alone produced more vehicles than all the Axis nations combined in 1938.

Having the knack for putting together a productive factory, Ford and GM began setting up factories in Japan, Germany, and across Europe to put the masses on wheels. Until 1936, the two controlled 90 percent of the Japanese auto market. When Japan began mobilizing its troops in China, it used Ford trucks. In Italy, Mussolini wouldn't give government permission for a Ford plant since he wanted all-Italian factories like Fiat. When the need for trucks to invade Ethiopia and Somalia arose, however, he ordered 2,200 trucks from Ford (and paid for 800 more, which Henry Ford refused to send).

Unbeknownst to Ford and GM in 1938, Hermann Goering demanded that the German-based factories of Ford-AG and GM Opel begin producing more trucks and war materiel. GM claimed that American workers at the Opel factory in Germany quit when hostilities broke out. Nevertheless, the factories, which gave the Axis many of its vehicles, were already in place.

Postwar, GM and Ford received reparations from the U.S. government for the bombing of their plants in Germany. What was left of the Opel plant the Soviets took back to Russia as war booty and to build vehicles for their use during yet another war against the U.S.: the Cold War. ∎

STRICTLY SUPER

I T'S a great day for our side whenever our flyers sweep out over the target in those fleets of B-29 Superfortresses.

Of course, Fisher Body does not make the complete Superfortress. But it does make huge dorsal fins, horizontal stabilizers, rudders, elevators and ailerons. Yes, and flaps, wing tips, outboard wings and turret parts, too.

More than that, Fisher Body makes engine nacelles — using more than 18,000 jigs and tools to turn out the 3,000 parts that are required for each nacelle.

Fisher Body is proud of its part in building this great Boeing-designed ship. All the skills and techniques inherent in the Fisher Body organization are concentrated on giving superworkmanship to the Superfortress. Yet it is but one of many war jobs including big guns, delicate aircraft instruments, tanks, and assemblies for other bombers.

And you may be certain that as long as war equipment is needed, the fine craftsmanship symbolized by the "Body by Fisher" emblem will keep right on backing up the courageous crews who pilot these great superplanes.

Every Sunday Afternoon
GENERAL MOTORS SYMPHONY OF THE AIR
NBC Network

DIVISION OF GENERAL MOTORS

Bombers for Peace
"V for Victory!" the little boy exclaims to his liberators. As far as equipment goes, however, the Axis often recognized its competitors' vehicles as superior. Hirohito zipped around in a 1935 Packard, and Rommel advised his troops, when they captured trucks, to keep only British-made Ford trucks, since they had better traction in the sand.

Censored!!
To demonstrate its patriotism, Pontiac willingly censored sensitive information to protect the troops. A sure eye-catching ad, since the reader inevitably tries to figure out the missing text.

Pontiac Reports to the Nation on Arms Production!

On April 30th, at 11:50 P.M., Pontiac delivered its ████th automatic anti-aircraft cannon to the United States Navy.

The contract covering this important war assignment called for the production of only ████ guns up to that date.

Thus, Pontiac deliveries of these vitally-needed weapons have exceeded the rate of production specified in the contract by 12 times and the time specification by 7 months.

ABLE TO disintegrate dive bombers with a spray of explosive shells, the ████████ cannon was once the handmade dream of a ████ ordnance wizard. Today, guns of the same type—*but officially recognized as better built and less expensive*—are being pressed into immediate service on the fighting ships of the U. S. Navy, the ████ Navy and on ████████ that sail the seven seas.

The attainment of volume production on this desperately wanted weapon is but one salient in Pontiac's production of arms. Concurrently, Pontiac men are at work on six *additional* assignments involving the elements of victory on land, afloat and in the air.

Assignment No. 2 calls for the production of a total of ████ ████ █ mm. anti-aircraft guns for the U. S. Army. In a █-acre plant, tooling is proceeding, *ahead of schedule,* which

calls for the delivery of the first gun before ████████ 1st. ████████

Far exceeding in complexity either of the foregoing is Pontiac assignment No. 3—one of the most complicated instruments of attack developed in the history of warfare. Comprising over 4300 separate parts, its production in quantity is a challenge which we at Pontiac have eagerly accepted. Previously, its maximum total production in this country was at a rate of only █ a month. According to schedule, we will be producing █ a day before ████████ 1st, 194█.

Supplementing these major activities are 3 others, widely different in character—each calling for special organization,

Awarded on January 20th, 1942, to PONTIAC for outstanding production of Navy ordnance.

facilities and personnel.

They involve respectively: the current production of ████ heavy-duty ████ engine inter-assemblies a month—which will be *quadrupled* in █ months; the manufacture of vital transport mechanisms at a rate of ████ a day; the production of █ large tank unit-assemblies a week in an especially tooled █-acre plant; and, finally, the crating each 24-hours for overseas shipment of ████ heavy-duty military vehicles being produced by an allied member of the General Motors family.

This is Pontiac's first report to the Nation on its progress to date in the production of arms for victory. In making it, we salute the men on the far-flung battle lines, to whose valor and self-sacrifice we all owe so much . . . and whose deeds serve as a constant inspiration to greater effort on our part.

Seeking to cooperate fully in the war effort, Pontiac has voluntarily censored this advertisement.

Pontiac DIVISION OF **General Motors**

WE'RE BUILDING ARMS FOR VICTORY

WAR AT HOME: ROSIE THE RIVETER TAKES CHARGE

As the war raged overseas, a Texaco poster on the home front threatened workers with an evil-looking Japanese rubbing his hands saying, "Go ahead, please—TAKE DAY OFF!" The drawings of Walt Disney were enlisted for a short cartoon clip in "Victory through Air Power," which Lockheed later used in serious ads to show the country its good work.

Those able to take car trips on the mere three gallons of gas that were rationed per week could see fervently patriotic Burma Shave signs such as, "LET'S MAKE HITLER/AND HIROHITO/ LOOK AS SICK AS/OLD BENITO."

On February 22, 1942, all production of cars not for the war effort was stopped. To save resources, gas and tires were rationed and a 35 miles per hour speed limit was enforced. In 1943, Oldsmobile urged citizens to "Convert your car into a VICTORY CAR!"

During the war, being a home mechanic became a point of pride. Teenagers gathered pieces of old cars and assembled jalopies, often missing the muffler to make the car quicker or at least *sound* faster.

By necessity, women became pressed into service as mechanics, since men were off fighting on the battlefield. The mantra of the day was illustrated in this ad copy: "Doing a Man's Job—training fighting men! Miss Elsa Gardner trains soldiers! . . . Her transportation is her 1935-model Oldsmobile." After years of ridicule, women drivers were finally deemed legitimate.

Farmers were also encouraged by car manufacturers through ads to produce for the war effort, as long as a vehicular product placement could find its way into the text. "America's Farmers are fighting the good fight . . . and Chevrolet cars and trucks are helping them to win the battle of food production," said a wartime magazine ad. Not just men were encouraged, as International Harvester trucks and tractors proclaimed, "Women join the 'Field Artillery' as International Harvester Dealers Teach Power Farming to an Army of 'Tractorettes.' "

Postwar, however, Rosie the Riveter was out of a job as returning G.I. Joes needed work. Car ads now focused on families as Joe and Rosie spawned the Baby Boomers. After all those frugal years of fixing up the car, it was time for a new one. ■

Hitler is My Co-Pilot
Car pools were considered a patriotic duty, as this 1942 poster indicates. Although the image shown here doesn't push a particular make, the idea of supporting your country by buying a car was passed down through the years. George Romney, who hoped to advance the idea of small cars as president of AMC, claimed in a 1958 ad that "[The Rambler] is much more than just 'another new car.' Each is a ringing declaration of *independence* for the U.S. motorist."

1942 Oldsmobile Service
Although keeping cars and trucks alive during the war was considered a patriotic duty, most materials were actually moved by rail. After the war, lobbyists for highways claimed that an Interstate highway system was crucial for defense. In 1956, the National System of Interstate and Defense Highways was encouraged by car ads pushing "transportation lines" and assuming these were automobile lines.

FOR VICTORY, BUY UNITED STATES WAR BONDS!

GUARDING
VITAL TRANSPORTATION LINES!

THOUSANDS OF OLDSMOBILE SERVICE
MECHANICS KEEP WATCHFUL CARE OVER CARS
THAT CANNOT BE REPLACED

IN a nation geared to a war-time tempo, transportation plays a vital role. Private cars and trucks, as well as the great public carriers, must be constantly on the job — carrying men to their machines, carrying materials of war to their many destinations. Oldsmobile service men take pride in the part they are playing in this "Battle of Transportation." They are devoting their skill, their experience and all their equipment to the job of protecting the supply lines that keep America strong.

Your own automobile is an essential part of this great transportation system. It is your patriotic duty to keep that automobile in condition. It must last, because it cannot be replaced. And it must not waste rubber, gasoline, or other key materials. Perhaps in the past you have managed to "get by" with only lubrications and oil changes — but today, lubrication alone is not enough. Today, you need lubrication plus adjustments — lubrication to retard wear, mechanical adjustments to compensate for wear and lengthen your car's life. Your Oldsmobile dealer offers just this type of *complete* service program. See *him*...and save your car...for yourself and for your country.

OLDSMOBILE SERVICE

AND SERVICE FOR ALL MAKES OF CARS

Now, whatever make you drive, you are invited to take advantage of your Oldsmobile dealer's high-quality service facilities.

OLDSMOBILE DEALERS of AMERICA
"IN SERVICE FOR THE NATION"

The colors are red, white and blue.

The cars are Limited Edition Impalas, Novas and Vegas.

They're the special Spirit of America Chevrolets arriving at your Chevy dealer's right now.

They're cars known for their value. Distinctly styled with special interiors and equipment. Packaged like no Chevrolet before. Available for a limited time only.

Get the Spirit at your Chevy dealer's while they last.

The Spirit of America Impala package: • White or blue exterior. • Special white padded vinyl roof. • Special striping. • Special white wheels with paint stripes and trim rings. • Spirit of America crests. • Dual Sport mirrors, LH remote-control. • Wheel-opening moldings and fender skirts. • Bumper impact strips. • White all-vinyl interior trim with blue or red accents and carpeting. • Deluxe seat and shoulder belts. • Quiet Sound Group body insulation.

The Spirit of America Nova package: • White exterior. • Black touring-style vinyl roof. • Special striping. • Spirit of America decals. • White rally wheels with trim rings and special hubs. • Black dual Sport mirrors, LH remote-control. • Black grille. • E78-14 white-stripe tires. • White all-vinyl bucket seat interior. • Red carpeting.

The Spirit of America Vega package: • White exterior. • White vinyl roof. • Special striping. • Spirit of America decals. • White GT wheels with trim rings. • Custom Exterior. • Black-finished body sills. • White LH remote Sport mirror. • A70-13 white-lettered tires. • White all-vinyl Custom Interior. • Red carpeting.

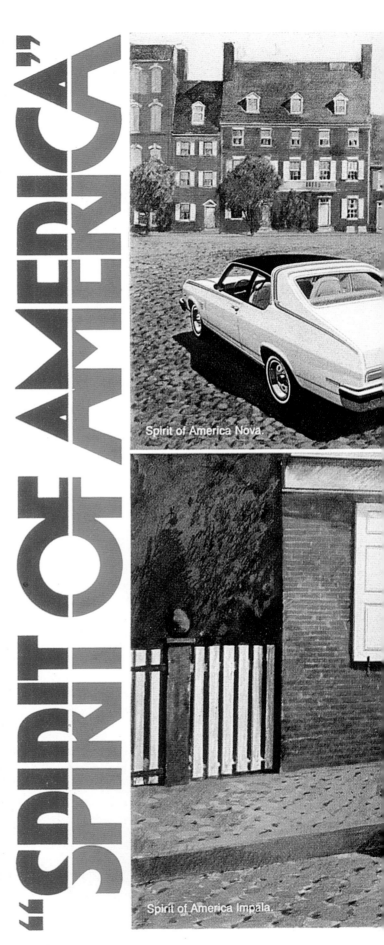

Spirit of America Nova.

Spirit of America Impala.

A limited edition of Chevrolets in America's favorite colors.

Spirit of America Vega.

NATIONAL DEFENSE AND DEFENSIVE NATIONALISM

While patriotism may have reached its peak during World War II, American automakers have always wrapped themselves in red, white, and blue. In 1928, for example, Packard bragged about the beautiful land in which an immigrant family could realize the American Dream making fine automobiles. After World War II, however, auto patriotism took on a new Cold War character.

The automobile was as American as military spending, urban sprawl, and union busting. When the 1956 Federal Interstate Highway Act was passed, automobile and commuter culture was dubbed vital to national defense. Proponents maintained that the decentralized, suburbanized cities were more difficult for the Ruskies to bomb into oblivion. President Eisenhower, thinking American V-8s needed an honest chance to outrun the H-bomb, argued, "In case of atomic attack on our key cities, the road net must permit quick evacuation of target areas."

Most of the time the glory of the United States goes without saying. But when its preeminence has been questioned, car manufacturers have been quick to sing its praises. The early years of the Cold War witnessed an explosion of auto-style American boosterism. Perhaps the craziest came from author John J. O'Neill, who proposed replacing American internal-combustion cars with "atomic automobiles!" "Each cylinder will contain a complete atomic power unit," he wrote days after the bomb fell on Hiroshima. "When the piston reaches the top of the cylinder, a small block of uranium 235 located like a central spark plug would be immersed in water, causing the atomic-energy chain reaction to burst into action." Car bomb! Major auto manufacturers must have ducked for cover when such visionaries came through the door, at the same time they touted their own versions of American ingenuity.

American car makers' patriotism reached fever pitch in the 1970s when their market share was threatened by foreign manufacturers of cheap, small cars. Watergate, Vietnam, and the OPEC oil embargo had proven America vulnerable, and car companies from Germany and Japan arrived to challenge the home teams. By the mid-1970s domestic sales had plummeted and storage lots were full of 1.6 million unsold automobiles. "American Made" was one of the few sales pitches U.S. manufacturers had left. Chrysler vowed, "America's not going to be pushed around anymore," in its ad for the Dodge K-Car—its first new model after its government bailout—and Pontiac's 1981 Grand Prix ads featured a dumbfounded Japanese businessman declaring, "Pontiac must have something we don't." Unfortunately, many Americans were more concerned about the cost of buying and running an auto than where it was made, and the home team fought to hold on. ∎

"Wartime"

World War II song from GM film:

"Listen GM soldiers,
And you're every one a soldier
in the Army of production
Fighting for our liberty.

Working at your benches
and machines you're in the trenches
of the arsenal of freedom
struggling for democracy.

Uncle Sam has set a job for you,
Folks of General Motors,
Let's tell Sam we're coming through.

Spread the news to Adolf
and the son of the Rising sun
Tell GM what we've done
then tell 'em we've just begun!
You ain't seen nothing yet!

Tanks—we'll keep 'em rolling!
Planes—we'll keep 'em flying!
Guns! Guns! Guns! Guns!
—we'll keep 'em shooting!
Give 'em hell!
On for America to build for victory!"

Betsy Ross Drove a Chevy!
Previous: During the 1973–1974 oil crunch, domestic carmakers relied on consumer patriotism to battle the incoming foreign compacts. Gearing up for the Bicentennial are the 1974 Nova, Impala, and Vega—the car whose automated construction at the GM Lordstown plant proved "American Made" did not necessarily mean made by Americans!

49ers
Harry Truman only received 49.5 percent of the popular vote in the 1948 Presidential election. He had nothing on the 1949 Ford, the center of this American-style hero's welcome. In reality, Ford ran a distant second to General Motors in the postwar sales race.

53

Has Nash Started a new Vogue in Motoring?

AT PALM BEACH! And at smart places everywhere, you'll see the people that other people copy stepping out in Nash cars this year!

From Actual Photograph of Nash Ambassador Six 4-Door Sedan with trunk

The swing to Nash grows stronger . . . thousands realize it's no longer smart to be _too_ thrifty . . . when you can get such big cars for so _little_ more than small cars cost!

● A few years ago it was the "style" to scrimp and save on the family automobile. But not this year. Thousands are getting out of the "small car" class. They are changing to Nash . . . stepping out in style again!

And never before have such big cars cost so little. The Nash La-Fayette-"400" is a great big 117-inch wheelbase car . . . much bigger than any of "all three" small cars. But compare prices on the 4-door sedan models. *You'll be astonished!* This big Nash costs just a few dollars more.

The Nash Ambassador Sixes and Eights are the last word in luxurious motoring. They're powered with "Twin Ignition" engines.

And all Nash cars give you over-sized hydraulic brakes, strong steel bodies, wide seats, extra headroom and legroom—*plus* those vital engineering features that make Nash cars run smoother and "sweeter" for years.

Go to your Nash dealer. See how much more Nash gives you for your money. Then you'll *know* why thousands are changing to Nash.

ON THE AIR! Floyd Gibbons as Master of Ceremonies with Vincent Lopez and Orchestra. Famous guest stars! C. B. S. stations coast to coast every Saturday, 9 P. M. EST. Tune in!

DELIVERED PRICES! *Get Nash delivered prices. Compare with others. See how Nash saves you money. Delivered prices throw a new light on the remarkable value Nash is offering this year. Easy budget plans. Terms low as $28 monthly. Automatic Cruising Gear available on all models at slight extra cost*

1937 X-RAY SYSTEM NOW READY!
The first complete summary available to the public of all the facts about all the new cars. Reveals some astonishing differences in cars of the same price. See it at any Nash showroom. Buy with your eyes open this year!

ASK ABOUT THE CONVENIENT TERMS AND LOW RATES AVAILABLE THROUGH THE NASH-C. I. T. BUDGET PLAN

NASH LaFAYETTE-"400"
117-inch wheelbase

NASH AMBASSADOR SIX
121-inch wheelbase

NASH AMBASSADOR EIGHT
125-inch wheelbase

STYLING

> *"My primary purpose for twenty-eight years has been to lengthen and lower the American automobile, at times in reality and always at least in appearance. Why? Because my sense of proportion tells me that oblongs are more attractive than squares."*
> —Harley Earl in 1954, from Alfred Sloan's My Years with General Motors

In 1899, the first stream-lined car was produced, La Jamais Content, with a sheet-metal body and electric engine to boot. It set a land-speed record of a whopping 66 miles per hour, and the streamlining race was on. Ferdinand Porsche took aerodynam-ics to heart as he tested the precursors to the VW Beetle for air resistance. The Chrysler Airflow of the same era claimed 40 percent less air resistance than other cars of the same year due to the uni-tized construction of its chassis and body.

While Streamline Moderne may have been the rage of everything from coffeemakers and prefab diners to automo-biles, this look of moder-nity didn't necessarily mean the cars drove more quickly, the diners made faster food, or the cof-feemakers speeded up your coffee. There was a vast difference between streamlining that could be seen and actual aerodynamics. Even so, this didn't stop GM from forming a styling department in 1925 to

Ever Forward
The Essex Supersix of 1927 advertised that "Riding is like Flying," previewing the impending jet age styling to come. By the 1950s, curved windshields twisted around the front of cars simulating a cockpit. The 1960 Ford T-Bird attached taillights to look like the flame exhaust of planes or rockets. This 1955 Dodge ad sums up Chrysler's Forward Look, always pushing faster while making the cars ever bigger.

Trend Setters
The streamlining on this 1937 Nash follows the fad of aerodynamics. So be like "the people that other people copy" and take off in a Nash. In 1958 Buick, whose front grille was dubbed the "dollar grin" in Europe, would follow the lead of these early models focusing on size, fashion, and flight writing, "Out of the Blue—the Big Breakthrough. It's the new face of fashion—the new feeling of flight. The Air Born B-58 Buick." *Steve Hanson Collection*

appeal to the public's lust for modernity.

Harley Earl designed GM's first mass-produced stylized car: the 1927 La Salle, complete with "Fly-ing Wing" fenders. For smoother lines in the design he made styling models out of clay instead of the traditional wood and metal. After World War II, he would go whole hog and base Cadillac design on the Lockheed P-38 twin-engine fighter plane. Chrysler and Ford had to follow Earl's lead to stay in business. The race for cars to look like planes was on. The 1949 Buick added side "venti-ports" ("mouse holes"), the 1950 Studebaker Cham-pion DXL countered with a pointed-nose hood and a grille cloning the front end of an airplane.

By the early 1950s, styling became more im-portant than actual mechanical breakthroughs. As GM President Alfred Sloan said, "The policy . . . was valid if our cars were at least equal in design to the best of our competitors in a grade, so that it was not necessary to lead in design or to run the risk of untried experiments." John DeLorean, a later GM exec, would mourn that customers only bought cars based on styling, or "the new wrinkles in the sheet metal," and that there were no impor-tant technological innovations since automatic transmission and power steering. Once again, form won over function. ■

FASHION: CONSPICUOUS CONSUMPTION

"Design these days means taking a bigger step every year. Our job is to hasten obsolescence. In 1934 the average car ownership span was five years; now it is two years. When it is one year, we will have a perfect score."
—Harley Earl, GM designer

★ ★ ★

In 1925, GM launched a design department in order to make its cars pleasing to the eye, not just functional tools. In doing so, GM was acknowledging that cars had moved well beyond the realm of mere utilitarian transportation. A 1929 Hupmobile ad summed up the fad as "the lifting force of fashion that now sweeps through every American home . . . changing our lives, our homes, our clothes, our cities . . . creating a thirst for new beauty and new charm."

Designers were commissioned by car manufacturers to add the fashion touch to their cars. "Hollywood Set by Chasen's, Star fashions by Maurice Rentner, Catalina Four-Door Hardtop by Pontiac," bragged a 1956 Pontiac ad. Eventually

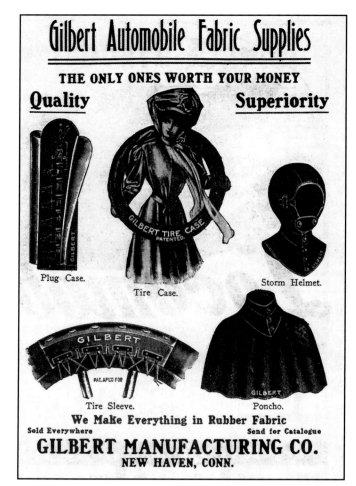

Automobile Clothing
Around the turn of the century, proper riding gear wasn't only a fashion accessory but also a necessity because of the lack of heating, the muddy conditions, breakdowns, and open cars. Helmets, goggles, turbans, and neck mufflers came in all sorts of styles and were made of exotic furs of rodents and marsupials such as the nutria and the wombat.

Matching Dress
Thirty years after the Nash ad, the idea is identical. It's all the same, whether it's "A few years ago it was the 'style' to scrimp and save on the family automobile. But not this year" of the 1937 Nash, or "Lots of people . . . go shop the most popular smaller cars and think, 'If these cost this much, imagine how much the big ones are!' The fact is they're in Chrysler territory" of the 1966 Chrysler. Fashion is worth the extra price.

CHRYSLER
Move up...Move now

**You're probably in the Chrysler class right now
—and don't even know it.**

designers such as Bill Blass, Halston, Pauline Trigere, and even Levi Strauss were designing special-edition autos.

The main focus of fashion marketing was women, as a 1940 Ford ad pointed out, "My husband knows all about engines and brakes but I'm the expert on *Style*! . . . We agreed on a Ford V-8." Or as a 1950s DeSoto ad advised that the extra-wide doors were "wonderful for party dresses and tight skirts."

In the following decades, outrageous two-tone color schemes came out of Detroit, such as Avalon Yellow and Raven Black or Bolero Red and Raven Black with gaudy chrome to separate the shades. The 1950s Dodge LaFemme in pink and charcoal gray even came with a matching pink umbrella and pink purse rack.

Since cars were fashion accessories, manufacturers encouraged women to match their car interiors to their jewelry and clothes. "Oh, Darling! It's so lovely that I haven't a thing to go with it," said a woman in a 1939 Ford ad. Cadillac ads featured expensive jewelry over its cars as the appropriate match to its luxury mobile. Even *Archie* comics portrayed Veronica Lodge as having a new car for each color of her fingernail polish.

In an effort to show women exactly what to wear in their automobile, a 1957 Pontiac ad promoted the "off-the-shoulder look" with a white and blue interior and "a dip on the seat to emulate the bare shoulder of the fashionable dresses of the time." A woman was pictured with a dress that matched the seats perfectly. Needless to say, the fashion would be updated the following year, making what GM's designer Harley Earl called "dynamic obsolescence." Alfred Sloan dubbed this the "constant upgrading of product," with the goal of eventually encouraging consumers to purchase a new General Motors car annually. ■

Auto's Big Brother: the Airplane
Early ads for luxury automobiles, such as this one from 1930, often featured planes, in the hope that a little of the cache of air travel would rub off on their product.

"People who Thunderbird move in a special atmosphere."
—1964 Ford ad

★ ★ ★

"Look out for those clouds! You're skimming straight for the horizon! Warm wind softly fans your face as you soar to the crest of the hill. And stretching below you are ribbons of roads and trees that dwindle to pencils. . . . Watch out—or you'll bump into one of those big, billowy clouds! You're driving a new Lincoln Zephyr, mister, and that means you're riding high!"

Generations of Detroit designers were unable to get their vehicles off the ground, but Madison Avenue pretended Chitty Chitty Bang Bang was in mass production. Year after year, advertisers used planes to sell cars.

Airplanes represented speed, power, and freedom in a way that no other vehicle could. The

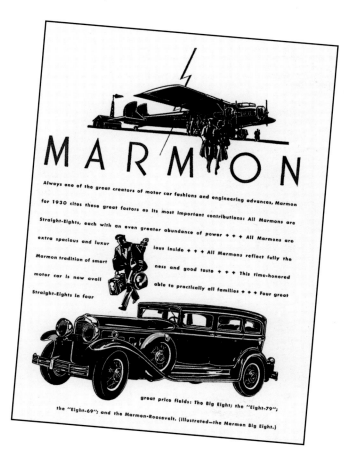

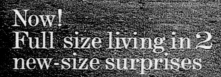

For '61
Buick brings you

THE CLEAN LOOK of action!

Le Sabre

Now!
Full size living in 2
new-size surprises

TURN THE PAGE AND SEE WHY '61 IS BUICK'S YEAR!

THE BEL AIR 4-DOOR SEDAN

Chevrolet's 3 new engines
put new fun under your foot!

You've got the greatest choice going in the Motoramic Chevrolet! Would you like to boss the new "Turbo-Fire V8" around . . . strictly in charge when the light flashes green . . . calm and confident when the road snakes up a steep grade? (Easy does it—you're handling 162 "horses" with an 8 to 1 compression ratio!) Or would you prefer the equally thrilling performance of one of the two new 6's? There's the new "Blue-Flame 136" teamed with the extra-cost option of a smoother Powerglide. And the new

"Blue-Flame 123" with either the new standard transmission or the extra-cost option of new Touch-Down Overdrive. See why Chevrolet is stealing the thunder from the high-priced cars? It has that high-priced, high-fashion look and everything good that goes with it—power, drives, ride, handling ease, *everything*. Let your Chevrolet dealer demonstrate how Chevrolet and General Motors have started a whole new age of low-cost motoring! . . . Chevrolet Division of General Motors, Detroit 2, Michigan.

Stealing the thunder from the high-priced cars! Motoramic **CHEVROLET**

Hey, Get Off the Runway!
The 1955 Bel Air commands attention in the presence of this marvel of Cold War military spending. Even the pilot in the cockpit is impressed.

train, with its immense, surging engines was unable to escape the confines of its track and its associations with mass transportation. Commuter traffic jams made it all too apparent that the automobile was also trapped in a two-dimensional grid of streets and highways. The military jet or private plane, on the other hand, went wherever the individual pilot desired—"the sky was the limit!"

The more literal-minded chose to picture their automobiles in close proximity to the latest models of airplanes, hoping some of the glamour and excitement of aeronautics would rub off on their earthbound products. Studebaker, for example, displayed its 1929 President Eight Roadster alongside a two-prop seaplane, insinuating that both were important beach accessories for the ultrachic. A startling number of advertisements featured car owners simply hanging out at airports, no luggage

Car as Plane
Auto body designers often took inspiration from the sleek lines and bulbous curves of jets and airplanes.

The Thunderbird Touch:
An overhead Safety Convenience Panel

1966 Thunderbird Town Landau

Delusions of grandeur or a problem with the exhaust system?
Car becomes plane as this "Highway Pilot" aims for the sun in his 1966 Thunderbird Town Landau.

in hand, no international travel plans. Drivers of the 1954 Chevrolet Bel Air and the 1955 Pontiac 870 found themselves more at home surrounded by planes than by other autos.

When merely parking the automobiles near jets and airplanes did not make sales take off, some ad copy claimed products were actually flying machines. One ad exclaimed, "Nothing without wings climbs like a '56 Chevrolet!" And after test-driving the 1962 "Jet-Smooth Chevrolet" and the 1963 Jetfire from Oldsmobile (with its exclusive "turbo-rocket V-8") one might still be tempted to ask, as a Buick ad suggested, "Should you have a pilot's license before you buy a Riviera?"

Flight, for much of the century, was only available to the wealthy. Cars gained instant status through association with private planes and other fashion accessories of the ultrarich. As commercial airlines grew rapidly in the 1960s and more Americans could afford air travel, passenger-plane style began to appear in advertisements. "If you've jetted cross-country lately, you'll know where we got the name 'Jet-lounge interiors' for the '64 Chevrolet." ∎

1961 Cadillac

Caddies were the vehicle on which Harley Earl originally introduced the weird and dubious trend of tail fins. Cadillac ad copy described its endless mobile as though describing the architecture of the Coliseum with fins dubbed, "gracefully arched rear fenders."

FINS AND FLIGHT SWEEP STYLING: THE FORWARD LOOK

GM's chief of design wandered through the Selfridge Air Force Base in 1941 checking out the Lockheed P-38 Lightning fighter and had a vision. He dreamed that perhaps one day cars-cum-hovercrafts would fly through the air and need the stability of fins for navigation. Some fin scholars credit the Douglas F-4D Skyray plane with the inspiration, but there is no question that Harley Earl was thinking about a fighter plane when he decided to put tail fins on Cadillacs in 1948.

The fins were openly ridiculed and openly praised. Being extremely sensitive to fickle consumers, Earl vacillated on keeping the fins on the 1949 Caddy, but ultimately left them on, leading to a styling revolution. Perhaps the public backslapping following the war and the subsequent obsession with airplanes allowed for this bizarre design quirk.

Within a couple of years, every major car manufacturer followed GM's lead, and the battle began in earnest when Chrysler's chief of design, Virgil Exner, produced some of the largest fins cars would ever wield. Chrysler's fins were originally deemed more "feminine"— that is until the much-touted "Forward Look," making Chryslers and DeSotos into jet pods with every street a landing strip. Earl followed with the extremely low (less than 50 inches in height) Le Sabre in 1951 inspired by the F-86 Sabre fighter jet with more than 60 gadgets on the dashboard to simulate a cockpit.

Other airplane styling cues, from wraparound windshields (which often warped vision) to Venti-Port exhaust ducts, appeared on 1950s-era cars; both were eventually discontinued. The wraparounds disappeared because of safety concerns, and the ducts "because a California high-school principal complained that some of his male students used those on his Buick to relieve themselves," as David Gartman claims in *Auto Opium*.

60

This baby can flick its tail at anything on the road!

DE SOTO FIREFLITE 4-DOOR SEDAN IN SEATONE BLUE AND WHITE

Take the wheel of a new De Soto, and pilot her out through traffic toward the open road. Before you turn your second corner, you'll know you're driving the most exciting car in the world today. Here are some of the reasons why:

New *Torsion-Aire* ride! You get an amazingly level ride with De Soto's new suspension—Torsion-Aire. You take corners without sway . . . stop without "dive."

New *TorqueFlite* transmission! Most advanced ever built. Gives a smooth flow of power, exciting getaway!

New *Triple-Range* push-button control! Simply touch a button and *go!* Positive mechanical control.

New *Flight Sweep* styling! The new shape of motion—upswept tail fins, low lines, and 32% more glass area.

New super-powered V-8 engines! De Soto engine designs are efficient and powerful! (Up to 295 hp.)

Drive a new De Soto before you decide. You'll be glad you did. De Soto Division, Chrysler Corporation.

Wide new price range . . . starts close to the lowest!

FIRESWEEP—big-value newcomer—priced just above the lowest. 245 hp

FIREDOME—medi-um-priced pace-maker—exciting performance. 270 hp

FIREFLITE—high-powered luxury—the last word in design and power. 295 hp

DE SOTO

. . . the most exciting car in the world today!

De Soto dealers present **Groucho Marx** in "You Bet Your Life" on NBC radio and TV

The battle of the fins and the swept-wing look began in earnest in 1957 with auto industry claims that they were an essential element to stabilize larger cars. In reality, fins only steadied a car at speeds well over 60 miles per hour, and even then the aerodynamic effect was probably negligible.

Some consumers dared question the designers, such as a Bishop Oxam, who asked in a 1958 issue of *Advertising Age*, "Who are the madmen who build cars so long they cannot be parked and are hard to turn at corners, vehicles with hideous tail fins, full of gadgets and covered with chrome, so low that an average human being has to crawl in the doors? . . ." Even Virgil Exner eventually admitted in *The History of Chrysler* that he'd "given birth to a Frankenstein." By 1962, fins had disappeared, and the flamboyance of the '50s was given up for the more staid designs of the 1960s. ■

THE CELESTIAL HIGHWAY: THE AMERICAN CAR WINS THE SPACE RACE

By the time the Soviet Union launched Sputnik 1 on October 4, 1957, American autos already had spent years among the stars. Recurrent images of rockets and space travel appeared in auto ads from the early 1950s: cars launched, took off, turbo-thrusted, and floated through the galaxy.

Since the 1920s, GM styling boss Harley Earl had been obsessed with the technology and design of flight. The streamlined bodies, bulbous intake vents, and wraparound windshields found on the latest military planes were quickly integrated into his auto designs. By the 1950s, aerospace technology had advanced dramatically, Earl had become the vice-president of styling for General Motors, and the tail fins he had copped from the Lockheed P-38 Lightning had become a standard feature of American auto design. Unfortunately, Earl's designs offered more of the sound and fury of rockets than their actual substance. His 1953 Corvette, for example, looked like it could break the sound barrier but had to make do with a rather pedestrian six-cylinder engine. Earl was adept at adopting the style of science (and the science of style), but like most stylists it wasn't up to him to make sure cars could rocket through suburban streets at warp speed.

Advertisers willingly took their cars where no one had gone before. While trapped in traffic jams on lowly planet Earth, drivers could recall advertising images and pretend they were traversing the Milky Way and exploring strange new worlds in their 1953 Roadmaster or blasting off in their "designed-like-a-missile" 1960 Chrysler. ■

Closer to the Stars
"Twin-Turbine Dynaflow" enabled the 1953 Buick Roadmaster to skate along this uncrowded highway of stars. Flowing lines and protruding fenders suggested aeronautic design. This ad made the metaphor explicit as the driver embarks on a commute that makes the jaunt from the suburbs look like visiting the neighbors.

Future Perfect
Cars in space found inspiration in sci-fi films as much as in military planes. This 1958 General Motors ad looks almost like an outtake from *Forbidden Planet*. These motorists bring American car culture to the outer limits, perhaps spreading the words of the film's hero: one "that cannot face the facts of the machine and mass production is predoomed to futility and petulance."

Never before a Lincoln so long...*and so longed-for!*

"Never before a Lincoln so long . . . *and so longed-for!*" blared the ad copy for this 1956 Premiere model. Ad agencies needed two pages of space to fit their huge cars on the pages of *Life,* while photographers used special "astigmatic" lenses to stretch the cars to eternity. The following year ad copy shouted, "No other car is so Lincoln long . . . Lincoln low . . . and Lincoln lovely!"

Rocket-Charged Oldsmobile

Copywriters for Oldsmobile may have found inspiration from the sci-fi films at the local theater. Ads for the make in the 1950s provide an encyclopedia of references to space travel, speed, and the future—all fired home with excessive, high-powered exclamation points!! Here are a few examples:

"Oldsmobile launches an all-time great, all new 'Rocket' Super 88!"
"Oldsmobile Rockets Ahead!"
"Brilliant 'Rocket' Engines!"
"Superb new 'Rocket Ride'!"
"Thrilling 'Rocket' Engine action!"
"Glamour star!"
"Action star!"
"Value star!"
"Starfire!"
"Glamorous new Futuramics!"
"Smart Futuramic styling!"
"POWER!"
"Power personality!"
"Oldsmobile's mighty 'Rocket' Engine sends you on your way with a flashing surge of power!"

OLDSMOBILE ROCKETS AHEAD !

Hydra-Matic Drive, at new reduced price, now optional on all Oldsmobile models.

63

presenting the value-packed

COMET 1961...*the better compact car*

...only compact car with fine car styling

...priced with or below the other compacts

The only compact with fine-car styling *A spirited sense of proportion gives Comet the most successful styling in the compact-car field. New rustproof aluminum grille, exquisite interior fabrics, new fine-car touches everywhere.*

The first family-size compact *Comet's 114" wheelbase (longer than any other compact's) provides spacious comfort other compacts sacrifice. There's no cramp in a Comet, even for six sizable grownups. In fact, Comet is the same size as the popular standard cars of just a few years ago. And there's trunk space for a family-size load of luggage besides . . . over 28 cubic feet.*

Big-car ride—small-car handling *The refined suspension (plus the 114" wheelbase) makes Comet's ride steadier and smoother than many standard cars. Still you'll find that Comet turns, parks and handles almost as easily as a baby carriage.*

Priced with or below the other compacts *For all its new fine-car flair, family-size comfort, big-car ride and extra value features, Comet is still priced with or below the other compacts.*

New Thrift Power 170 engine for '61 *Comet now offers two economy engines—the standard Thrift Power Six plus the new optional Thrift Power 170 for 11% faster highway passing, 22% better acceleration.*

Choose from two- and four-door wagons, too
With cargo space you'd expect from larger-size wagons (over 76 cubic feet!) and retractable rear window for easier loading, a Comet wagon is one of the most efficient on the road. See Comet . . . the No. 1 for '61...at your Mercury-Comet dealer's

LINCOLN-MERCURY DIVISION *Ford Motor Company*, BUILDERS OF FINER CARS OF EVERY SIZE FOR EVERY PURPOSE
LINCOLN CONTINENTAL...Nothing could be finer · MERCURY...The better low-price car · COMET...The better compact car

Comet Compact
Following the introduction of the Beetle, the Big Three began making their version of compacts. Even though they were claimed to be "priced with or below the other compacts," they couldn't match the Beetle's price, size, or popularity. Now Ford boasted, "Big-car ride—small-car handling" rather than the earlier big car feel that was supposed to entice customers.

GOOD THINGS IN SMALL PACKAGES: BEETLEMANIA!

"Many small cars give you a trunk the size of a hat box. A Nova's trunk holds one man's two-suiter, one lady's pullman, three overnight bags, one train case, one set of golf clubs, odds and ends."
—*1968 Chevy II Nova ad*

★　★　★

In the 1950s, a funny-looking vehicle crossed the Atlantic and eventually took the U.S. market by storm. With a simple ad headline of "Think Small," the VW Beetle soon was here to stay. The Big Three, however, took their time recognizing the success of the Bug, continuing instead to build the much more profitable behemoths for which they were famous.

While AMC President George Romney moaned to Congress about the "dinosaur in the driveway," which made sense since he was the head of a company already committed to making small cars, Detroit's Big Three paid scant notice. In fact, it wasn't until 1960, after the recession of 1958, that Ford, GM, and Chrysler took note and started building "compacts."

The domestic compacts of the 1960s were still pretty big compared to the Beetle, and it took the oil crisis of the early 1970s to truly shrink the dinosaurs. By the end of 1973, sales of small cars surpassed "standard-size" cars. Up until that time, Detroit had told the public that soon all cars would be minuscule, so people should get your land yacht while they still could. AMC's persistence in making compact cars, like its Pacer and Gremlin, helped make it the only company to show a sales increase at the beginning of 1974. At this point, even GM began to make petite automobiles. ■

Unique in Concept

Ramblers are unique. Here's how they compare in size with the average 1958 U. S. car and average European "small car"—

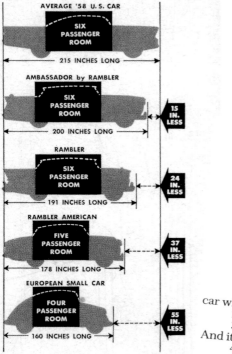

AVERAGE '58 U.S. CAR
SIX PASSENGER ROOM
215 INCHES LONG

AMBASSADOR by RAMBLER
SIX PASSENGER ROOM
200 INCHES LONG
15 IN. LESS

RAMBLER
SIX PASSENGER ROOM
191 INCHES LONG
24 IN. LESS

RAMBLER AMERICAN
FIVE PASSENGER ROOM
178 INCHES LONG
37 IN. LESS

EUROPEAN SMALL CAR
FOUR PASSENGER ROOM
160 INCHES LONG
55 IN. LESS

"New Rambler American Challenges 'Big Car Concept'"
The big guns at AMC were called out as early as 1958 against the increase in car size resulting in pinched pennies from gas hogs. In a statement from George Romney, then AMC president, he declared, "This iron mold, this 'big car complex,' is being smashed by the modern, efficient, compact Rambler, first introduced in 1950." After all, if the economic-minded consumer only "has two options—the small European car or a Rambler," what red-blooded American wouldn't choose the car that "is a ringing declaration of *independence* for the U.S. motorist." This graph was used to highlight the difference between the 1958 Rambler American and other makes.

The Gremlin in the Machine circa 1973
While the Pacer and the Gremlin may be a running joke among car buffs, both cars were moderate successes for AMC.

Anatomy of a Gremlin

1. Gremlin is the only little economy car with a standard 6-cylinder engine.
2. Reaches turnpike speed easily.
3. Weighs more than other small cars. And its wheels are set wider apart.
4. Has a wider front seat.
5. A wider back seat.
6. And more headroom in the trunk. And only American Motors makes this promise: The Buyer Protection Plan backs every '73 car we build. And we'll see that our dealers back that promise.

Buckle up for safety.

AMERICAN MOTORS BUYER PROTECTION PLAN
1. A simple, strong guarantee, just 101 words! When you buy a new 1973 car from an American Motors dealer, American Motors Corporation guarantees to you that, except for tires, it will pay for the repair or replacement of any part it supplies that is defective in material or workmanship. This guarantee is good for 12 months from the date the car is first used or 12,000 miles, whichever comes first. All we require is that the car be properly maintained and cared for under normal use and service in the fifty United States or Canada, and that guaranteed repairs or replacement be made by an American Motors dealer.
2. A free loaner car from almost every one of our dealers if guaranteed repairs take overnight.
3. Special Trip Interruption Protection.
4. And a toll free hot line to AMC Headquarters.

AMC ▟ Gremlin
We back them better because we build them better.

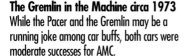

65

"It is true that only a big car can give you big car performance and comfort—you know it, everybody knows it. . . . It's a real automobile—a big car."
—1933 Pontiac Straight 8 ad

★   ★   ★

Critics claimed that large autos would bring down the entire auto industry in late 1950s. Even a representative of the AMA claimed that it made no sense to have "two tons of automobile to transport a 105-pound blond." But too much had been invested in widening streets across the country to make way for the behemoths. The city of Chicago alone spent $340 million between 1910 and 1940 to stretch its streets.

A 1940 Body by Fisher ad featured quintuplets mesmerized by a car hollering "So-o BIG!" Meanwhile, by 1949 AAA was protesting the huge size of cars and their extravagant styling. The auto industry, on the other hand, maintained that consumers wanted acres of chrome. Then in the 1950s, a bug-shaped mobile crossed the Atlantic and took America by storm. The VW Beetle lacked the extravagance but offered the economy that the titanic U.S. cars lacked.

Detroit ignored the bug and kept building bigger and better cars; luxury cars offered a much larger profit margin than compacts. "More room inside . . . without raising the roof or stretching the car," boasted a 1960 Dodge ad. Then in the early 1970s, the unthinkable happened: an oil crisis hit. Two strikes, and Detroit punted. Smaller cars took the game. ■

Anne Fogarty, famous fashion designer, drives a De Soto Sportsman.

DRIVE A | DE SOTO | BEFORE YOU DECIDE

There is no word in the English language that quite describes the utter satisfaction, the thrill, the delightful ease of driving a De Soto. Here is a car that translates your wishes into action almost with the speed of thought itself. There is an eager, natural response that is quite different from anything you're likely to find in other cars. That is why it is really important that you "drive a De Soto before you decide!" Your De Soto dealer will be delighted to have you take a turn at the wheel of either a Firedome or Fireflite. De Soto Division, Chrysler Corporation.

DE SOTO-PLYMOUTH dealers present **GROUCHO MARX** in "YOU BET YOUR LIFE" on NBC Radio and TV

DeSoto the Great

So long the fins don't even fit on the page. . . . The upward diagonal plus the white paint on the side converge in the front giving the perspective that this car is at least the length of a football field of chrome, whitewalls, and pure Firedome Hemi V-8 power. Although the white gloves, yellow print shirt, and dyed gray bangs aren't essential fashion accessories, like a two-tone DeSoto they require the driver to have a certain flair for the 1950s like this "famous fashion designer" in her DeSoto Sportsman.

Filippo Tommaso Marinetti became the father of a new art movement when he published his "Manifesto of Futurism" in 1909. The Italian poet and painter railed against the softness and complacency he believed characterized 19th-century Romanticism. He, instead, preached for the masculine power and vitality he found at the root of recent innovations in physics, technology, and the arts. The rip-snorting speed of the motorcar and airplane, and the pace of modern cities offered humans a means of escaping the drab, pathetic lives they had for centuries been leading. Tradition, liberalism, and sleepy immobility were out. They were to be violently replaced by innovation, "feverish insomnia," and the beauty of the machine. Marinetti embraced the technology of the 20th century, making it the center of his philosophy, politics, and personal style.

Marinetti's rants caught the ear of a young Benito Mussolini. The future *Duce* used the manifesto as the artistic foundation for Italian fascism. His words also must have made quite a stir among ad agency copywriters as well. The unashamed exaggerations and celebrations of the new found in Marinetti's writing were startlingly similar to a lot of the purple prose coming from Madison Avenue. One wonders if the futurist moved to New York, changed his name, and began working as an advertising copywriter. Here are a few examples for your perusal. You be the judge! ■

MODERN LIVING GOES FORWARD

NEW 1953 LINCOLN–POWERED TO LEAVE THE PAST FAR BEHIND

Futurist Manifesto

Auto advertisers' excitement about the future rivaled that of futurist artist F. T. Marinetti. The Italian futurists had fetishes for power, speed, airplanes, style, and continuous change. So did Detroit and Madison Avenue. This 1953 Lincoln Capri adhered to the "spirit that dares to defy the outworn tradition of bulk and fussy glitter." Was that purple prose written by Marinetti or an ad man? Only the fine print holds the answer!

F. T. Marinetti, Futurist

"Speed = scorn of obstacles, desire for the new and unexplored."

"Vertical takeoff. Tilting away from everyday life. The line of artistic power ever ascending."

"Against practicality we Futurists disdain the example and admonition of tradition in order to invent at any cost something *new*."

"Why should we look back, when what we want is to break down the mysterious doors of the Impossible?"

"We say that the world's magnificence has been enriched by a new beauty; the beauty of speed."

"We must shake the gates of life, test the bolts and hinges."

About his cars: "We went up to the three snorting beasts, to lay amorous hands on their torrid breasts."

"Soon machines will constitute an obedient proletariate of iron, steel, and aluminum at the service of men"

"We want no part of it, the past."

"Time and space died yesterday."

★　★　★

Automobile Ad Copy

"Nash is eager to take you to those unspoiled secret places, where road and hills keep other cars away!" —1939 Nash ad

"Smooth and straight as an arrow, without weaving or hesitation, you shoot forward on your way." —1939 Nash ad

"The people of the Pontiac Motor Division are never content with the commonplace, never hemmed in by the hackneyed. This is why you will receive a delightfully fresh point of view from the ownership of a 1960 Pontiac." —1960 Pontiac ad

"Yesterday is dead, today is gloriously alive, tomorrow calls clamorously for greater and greater endeavor!" —1953 Lincoln ad

"You've found new beauty, new grace, a rocketing new pace that makes you want to get up and go places."

"The absence of rattles tells you plenty." —1958 Body by Fisher ad

"Advanced Thrust that places the rip-snorting Wildcat V-8 engine far forward over the front wheels. Hurry down to your Buick dealer's and drive this torrid new BUICK!" —1962 Buick ad

"You'll find it amiably obedient. A softer suspension makes it responsive, quick and easy to take direction." —1959 Pontiac ad

"New 1953 Lincoln—powered to leave the past far behind." —1953 Lincoln ad

"The Futura is now." —1978 Ford ad

★　★　★

Into the 21st Century!
"Swiftly over the curves of the earth." In 1948, Oldsmobile unleashed the Futuramic, a car so "exciting and new" it needed a new word to describe it!
Steve Hanson Collection

FUTURAMIC

OLDSMOBILE

History is in the making at Oldsmobile. In celebration of the fifty years just past ... in anticipation of even greater years ahead ... America's oldest motor car manufacturer is now swinging into production on the first of an entirely new cycle of superlatively fine cars— *the Futuramic Oldsmobile.* Here is a car so new and exciting, it requires a brand new word—*Futuramic*—to describe it. A car with styling so daring and dramatic, it's just as modern as Oldsmobile's Hydra-Matic Drive. A car so advanced and ahead of the times it heralds the dawn of a new Golden Era in Oldsmobile's history. Watch for the 1948 Futuramic Oldsmobile at your Oldsmobile dealer's.

CELEBRATING OLDSMOBILE'S GOLDEN ANNIVERSARY

The car that's going places

with the Young in Heart

Aerodynamic Plymouth '56

Plymouth Belvedere 4-door Hardtop Sport Sedan. 28 other models. Furs by Maximilian.

Dream car...dream deal!

Women love this dream car...and, with a vital stake in family budgets, love the "dream deal" that Plymouth dealers offer...making it easy to own an all-new Plymouth '56...with wide doors that never snag frocks...generous headroom, so hairdos stay beautifully in place...rich fabrics...and utmost safety for the children...plus Push-Button Driving...only on Plymouth in the field!

Get the news: "PLYMOUTH NEWS CARAVAN" with John Cameron Swayze, NBC-TV. "SHOWER OF STARS" and "CLIMAX!" CBS-TV.

SEX AND SECURITY

"Ads are not meant for conscious consumption.
They are intended as subliminal pills for the subconscious
in order to exercise an hypnotic spell."
—Marshall McLuhan, 1964

"At the first sign of depression or a closed-in feeling,
take one of these Fairlane capsules. Acts fast.
Suitable for the entire family."
—1966 Ford ad

In the 1950s advertising seemed to discover Sigmund Freud. Copywriters couched the art of the sale in the language of psychology. "Motivational research" became the buzzword of the industry. Champions of the new method believed that consumers were not interested in buying a car. They wanted to satisfy their inner desires. "We no longer buy oranges, we buy vitality. We do not buy just an auto, we buy prestige," explained one executive. The automobile became a pleasantly distorting mirror—looking into the shiny chrome fender, the consumer saw the person he or she wanted to be.

Advertisers shifted their attention from the features of the cars they were selling to the emotional needs of the people they wanted to reach. Humans became the center of many advertisements, and their automobiles were moved to the sidelines. Detractors complained that consultants with Viennese accents could get rich telling copywriters what a car symbolized in psycholog-

A Mercury is to see yourself in

A Mercury is a lot of glittering moments

A Mercury reflects you

A Mercury is power shined up to GO

Everything in a Mercury is sweet and low— low upkeep, sweet feel

A Mercury is the Big **M** — one of the Ford family of fine cars

Because we make so many there's more for you in every car we make

Every garage should have at least one —— the Ford · the Thunderbird · the Mercury · the Lincoln · the Continental Mark II

The Inner Child in the Driver's Seat
Motivational research of the 1950s claimed that people bought automobiles to satisfy their psychological longings. Looking into the shiny chrome fender, the consumer saw himself as he wanted to be.

ical terms. A 289-cubic-inch engine meant virility. A wide wheelbase equaled confidence. Strength, excitement, youth, warmth, attitude— the car could provide them all. But above all else, motivational researchers contended, the car could grant the two things that every American desired but could not find: sex and security.

The fact is that advertisers had been filling people's emotional needs for a long time. Sex had been used as a selling point ever since flappers gave that "come-hither" look from the passenger seat of a Model A. Motivational research gave a scientific logic to this kind of appeal. It also marked a shift toward the unconscious. Double meanings in ad copy abounded as ads tried to subliminally appeal to buyers' unspoken desires. The consumer might not admit that he was interested in sex, but the advertiser knew better. Oedipal impulses, oral fixations, and general listlessness could all be treated by Dr. Feelgood, the local Chevy salesman. Car payments were cheaper than weekly therapy sessions, and an auto looked better than a stuffy analyst parked in a driveway. They were even more effective than Valium for beating away the blues of the Atomic Age. They were the perfect prescription for the inner child in the driver's seat. ■

Women's Dreams Interpreted
The dream? An interior large enough to accommodate frocks and bouffants! With furs, rockets, tail fins, the "young at heart," child safety, "Push Button Driving," and couples in love, this ad could make even Freud throw in the towel. But even he could not resist that ultrachic upholstery.

"A man may dream of inserting a key in a lock or wielding a heavy stick. Each of these can be regarded as sexual allegory. The real task is to understand why *the key has been preferred to the stick."*
— Carl Jung

"Take this key. Your key to a greater value.
Your key to a General Motors car."
—1951 GM ad

★ ★ ★

Sigmund Freud thought dreams represented people's repressed fears and desires. His pal Carl Jung believed dreams were the passageway to the collective unconscious. Harley Earl, styling guru at General Motors, thought dreams were the cars of tomorrow.

Earl and his design team created extravagant, experimental autos, then had them built out of steel and fiberglass. The "dream cars" were unveiled at extravagant "Motoramas," complete with dancers and live music, in order to test the novel designs against public scrutiny. The first successful "Motorama" graduate to go into mass production was the 1953 Corvette. When most got behind the wheel of that sleek, little auto, they realized that Earl's "dreams" concerned looks and style far more than engineering.

Even before General Motors gave Earl the nod to bring his fantasies to life, other manufacturers were in the dream-fulfillment business. The LaFayette Motors Company claimed in 1921, "You have always known there would be such a car." Another ad stated in 1940, "A driver's dream come true is the superb new Mercury 8." After the oil crisis and recessions of the early 1970s, Buick appeased consumers whose heads were no longer in the clouds with a "down-to-earth dream car," the 1978 Regal. Yet the carmaker's slogan clearly stated the industry's long-held formula for success: "A little science. A little magic." The skillful combination of the two—in either car or ad design—could successfully get consumers to follow Cadillac's 1970 advice to "stop dreaming and start living!" ■

Dream Machine
General Motors displays its 1953 "dream cars." Harley Earl and his styling team created experimental cars and unveiled them at extravagant Motoramas. No, you could not buy these at your local dealer, but these pictures were tempting enough to get you into the showroom anyway.

MY CAR MADE ME DO IT

"Outer beauty reflects inner quality."
—*1935 Chevrolet ad*

★   ★   ★

"**W**e have adequate proof in our case histories that people experience cars as personalities," Ernest Dichter told Chrysler in 1940, "as symbol of their own personalities, as expression of their own power and abilities, even as their own arms and feet." He then posed the challenge, "Tell me how a man drives, and I will tell you what kind of man he is." That may sound like a neat trick, but everyone already knew that a car defined its owner.

Ads constantly encouraged the idea that a car was a reflection of the driver's individual character. The auto was not just a means of transportation but a résumé on wheels, silently (or not so silently) exclaiming what made the driver special to the country-club or singles-bar set. Many early ads suggested that proper personalities were characterized by an almost unhealthy restraint, a fear of being gaudy. In 1929, a Studebaker declared the "soundness of your judgment," and the Dodge Senior Roadster was perfect for those "whose personal belongings invariably [were] distinctive as well as correct." Like a pair of well-polished spats and a tasteful kerchief in the suit pocket, the car presented a character of distinguished respectability.

In the 1920s, automobiles became available to a much wider segment of the American population. Similarly, as more models and colors were featured, advertisers maintained that there was a car for any and every personality. Cars became less a way of fitting in than expressing one's individuality. Paige offered "motor cars that match milady's mode—yes, her every mood!" "It's smart to be different!" exclaimed Chrysler in 1941, "Give your individuality free rein!" In 1961, Chevrolet could boast, "Chevy can match your personality . . . and then some!"

Cars did more than reflect one's personality. They *made* it! The 1924 Chevy was more than a car; it was a "personality multiplier." Those that lacked that vital "force of character" could simply hop into the Oldsmobile Super 88, "the car with the power personality!" The schizophrenic could enjoy the "split personality" of the 1963 Buick Riviera—one favored looks, the other performance. The wondrous 1965 Mustang promised it could turn a "born loser" into a winner every time. The metaphysical distinction between the personality of a car and that of its owner was so confused by 1972 that one ad frantically asked, "Do people own Cadillacs because they get more out of life, or do people get more out of life because they own Cadillacs?" ∎

Sidney spent Sundays seashelling at the seashore. Then Sidney started digging the '68 Mustang—the great original. Dug the models: hardtop, fastback and convertible. Liked the low price, too, which left Sidney lots of clams to design his own Mustang, Sidney style. Now Sidney's making waves all over. Last week he saved 3 bathing beauties. (And they all could swim better than Sidney!)

Only Mustang makes it happen!

FACTS ABOUT THE 1968 MUSTANG: Mustang's list of standard equipment can't be matched by any other sporty car in its price range. Includes four-mounted stick shift with fully synchronized 3-speed transmission, bucket seats, door-to-door carpeting, all-vinyl trim, 5-pod instrument cluster. And Mustang gives you a range of options no competitor offers. Like SelectShift with 3 forward speeds—can be used as a manual or an automatic, available with any model, any engine. Or an all-pushbutton AM Radio/Stereosonic Tape System. V-8's up to 390 cu. in. And the broadest choice of performance options around: including a special heavy-duty suspension, front power disc brakes on all models, wide-oval tires, and more.

FORD
. . . has a better idea

A Car with
Force of Character . . .

DODGE BROTHERS SENIOR
⊕ CHRYSLER MOTORS PRODUCT

Car Character
Autos possessed personalities of their own. The 1929 Roadster shared its owner's "force of character."

Personal Transformation
The 1968 Ford Mustang fastback had the power to magically transform a pathetic dweeb into a man so vital he wore "Life" on his chest!

FOUNTAIN OF YOUTH

*"The young people of our world
are turned on and tuned in to life.
To its mood and music. To its adventure and excitement.
And they're turned on in a real and honest way."*
—1969 Chevrolet ad

★   ★   ★

Ponce de Leon was right! The fountain of youth could be found in the New World. He was just a few centuries too early and a thousand miles south of Detroit.

Out of the primordial ooze of molten steel rose that city's phoenix—the solution to the age-old problem of old age. Humans spend the first and last years of their lives wrapped in the security that only diapers can provide. The years in between consist of rebelling against those swaddling clothes and longing for their return. The right automobile, ads suggested, could assist each stage.

The car could be a womb on wheels. Nestle into the plush seat of the 1968 Chrysler Imperial. You are completely in the care of this machine, its ad promised. Auto-temp control adjusts to a cozy 98.6, and the AM/FM tunes itself. "On long drives, set the optional Auto-Pilot speed control, readjust the seat, assume a new position. Relax. The tensions of mind and muscle are soon forgotten." The car took care of everything. It was the perfect parent for those who longed to be very young again.

For those whose nostalgia ran toward the teens rather than the prenatal, other cars offered the ideal ride. It was difficult to live up to the Technicolor memory of youth—drag races, hanging out at the neighborhood observatory after dark, getting bailed out by Dad. Many advertisements promised a youth better than consumers had actually lived. Cars vowed the virility, eagerness, and excitement that everywhere was associated with the young. No one said it better than the inspired copywriter who penned these words for the 1940 Lincoln Zephyr: "These sleek, powerful thoroughbreds—packed with hair-trigger get-up-and-go are youth's dream of what a perfectly poised and appointed fine car should look like, be, and do. And that goes also for every man Jack who dares never to grow old; for this is the car Ponce de Leon would choose—youthful, rugged, able, yacht-smart in all details, with a he-car capacity to go places and do things." In two years he was probably president of the agency.

Visions of youth changed according to the times. By the late 1960s, ads tried to incorporate the language of the youth movement. One could rebel in a new Rebel from American Motors. Or join the sexual revolution in a Plymouth Scamp. Advertisers often played catch-up with youth culture, not able to change their image as fast as the teens the ads invoked. This was unimportant, however. They were selling youth not to the young but to those who longed to be. A few months after the riots outside the 1968 Democratic convention, Chevrolet asked "what the younger generation is coming to." It then assured its middle-aged reader that the manufacturer was reasonable. "Don't think for a minute we won't sell you a Camaro if you're over thirty. After all, its not how young you are. It's how old you aren't." ■

"Real Cool!"
Right: The prosperity of the mid-1950s came too late for those whose teens had been consumed by the Great Depression and World War II. The 1954 Chevrolet Bel Air promised them a second chance. Only this time they had the cash to make a real impression! Many such ads sold youth not to the young but those who longed to be.

The Kids Are Alright
Following: While Students for a Democratic Society have decried "improved gadgets" and "the idolatrous worship of things by man," and the Student Non-violent Coordinating Committee risked their lives to register Southern black voters, Ford had a different definition of the youth movement in this 1964 ad.

Ever see a prettier car than the Chevrolet Bel-Air Sport Coupe? And this is just one of a great line of Chevrolet beauties. Best choice in the field.

You're only young <u>twice</u>!

Once when you take your first battered old jalopy to your heart . . . and once again when you put your first brand-new Chevrolet on parade!

WHAT'S CHEVROLET GOT THAT YOUNG PEOPLE GO FOR?

First of all: It's smooth! Real cool! It looks as a car ought to look that's loaded with youngsters who love the feel of a spirited pick-up and the power of broad-shouldered brakes. Chevrolet is the <u>only</u> low-priced car in the world with a Fisher Body.

And what a pleasant surprise to discover that you can run the new Chevrolet with the kind of money that fits a young man's budget. And, of course, everybody knows that Chevrolet's original cost is less than any other line in the low-price field.

It's the only low-priced car with a full length box-girder frame for *extra safety*.

But if you're interested in those new automatic power features a *family* car ought to have, you'll find that Chevrolet offers them all—optional at extra cost if you want them.

Why don't you drop around to your dealer's and take a ride in a new Chevrolet? . . . Chevrolet Division of General Motors, Detroit 2, Michigan.

YEAR AFTER YEAR MORE PEOPLE BUY CHEVROLETS THAN ANY OTHER CAR!

SYMBOL OF SAVINGS

CHEVROLET

EMBLEM OF EXCELLENCE

Ford Motor

a youth movement.

Company is:

The introduction of the '65 Mustang gave whole families a license to be young.

Now, everywhere you look, we're serving up more young ideas in our '65 cars: new disc brakes, livelier engines, 3-speed automatic transmissions across the line, new fresh air ventilation with windows closed—even *reversible* keys.

Our cars not only look, feel, and act young— they'll stay young.

Because of one old idea we never forget: <u>quality.</u>

The young ideas come from... Ford

MUSTANG · FALCON · FAIRLANE · FORD
COMET · MERCURY
THUNDERBIRD · LINCOLN CONTINENTAL

MOTOR COMPANY

AUTOEROTICISM

"A realist might say that a young lady is more likely to arouse thoughts of love than an automobile," speculated a 1955 Chevrolet ad. "But it would be obvious to the informed that a realist with such a literal outlook had never commanded a new Motoramic Chevrolet with a 'Turbo-Fire V-8' (or with one of the new 6s) under its bonnet!" The automobile has long been associated with sex, both as a place to engage in it and, especially in advertisements, a substitute for it. With date in tow, the car could make it up to "Inspiration Point." If the driver was alone, many cars were sleek, beautiful, and powerful enough to give new

meaning to autoeroticism. The owner of the 1939 Nash could reputedly enjoy the best of both worlds. Not only did the popular Nash convertible bed give the auto the nickname "the young man's model," but its driver could be prosecuted under the Mann Act in the car that was "long and lithe and radiant as a sixteen-year-old in her swim suit!"

Fetishization of the "curvaceous body lines," "sinewy bulges," and "obliging power" of automobiles proved an outlet for male sexual fantasies that were otherwise contained by puritanical repression and official censorship. Legions of sexual metaphors wormed their way into car ads. The members of design teams and copywriting departments were long on poetic license and very short on shyness. One could enjoy the thrilling, new "rhythmic ride" of the 1929 Olds, or wait until 1965 for the "tingling-with-anticipation" Starfire. The 1970 Buick could "light your fire," while the 1974 Thunderbird urged you to "make a little thunder of your own." Some ads were blatant, others more subtle, but they all paid tribute to the old advertising adage that "sex sells."

A few set out to determine how and why it sells. Ernest Dichter, a pioneer of motivational research, was hired by Chrysler in 1939 to find out why the manufacturer sold fewer convertibles than sedans. It seems many men were drawn into the showroom by the eye-popping convertibles, but once there they opted for the more pedestrian models. In his now famous report, Dichter determined that men thought of the convertible as they would a mistress, but the sedan as a wife. The first excited the male customer with dreams of freedom, adventure, and passionate sex. Once the time came to buy, however, the man made the same decision as when he married the girl next door and bought the practical auto. "Symbolically, he marries the sedan," a spokesman for Dichter concluded. The researcher encouraged Chrysler to continue pushing the sexy convertibles even though they only represented 2 percent of sales. Did the manufacturer take the advice? In 1955, the manufacturers promoted the Windsor Newport as, "18 gleaming feet of power waiting to call you master!" ■

This is Caprice Custom Coupe with roof styling unlike any other car's, with side view mirror and seven other standard safety items.

The Chevrolet "convertible" that doesn't convert

Clever. The vinyl roof covering available for your Caprice Custom Coupe creates the impression it's a convertible. But Caprice is really a luxurious hardtop with all the advantages of Chevrolet hardtop design. Inside, Caprice allows only luxury, like foam-cushioned seats, thick carpeting and paneling to highlight doors. Padded dash and seat belts, front and rear, for added safety. Want to top the Caprice? That's easy. Just tell us whether you want the black or beige vinyl roof cover.

CHEVROLET *Caprice* UNIQUE THE CHEVROLET WAY **GM**
Chevrolet Division

The Iconic Woman on Wheels
When she's not lounging on top of cars, she's a brain surgeon. A spokesman for motivational researcher Ernest Dichter once said, "If we get a union between the wife and mistress—all we sought in a wife plus the romance, youth, and adventure we want in a mistress—we would have, lo and behold, the hardtop!" This 1966 Caprice apparently had it all.

Bright Red Inside and Out
A gearshift standing at attention and ready to smoothly slip into drive. An obviously euphoric woman beckons with arms outstretched. The 1961 Starfire gave new meaning to "adventure in motoring excitement!"

Announcing...a new
high-performance
limited-edition
sports convertible

Starfire

by OLDSMOBILE

Spectacular! Top-grain leather interior . . . with contoured bucket seats.

Adventure in Motoring Excitement!

Standard Equipment: Sports-type control console • Tachometer • Hydra-Matic with stick control • Power windows • Power steering • Power brakes • Power seat • Starfire Engine with ultra-high compression ratio • 440 lb-ft. torque at 2800 r.p.m. • 330 H.P. at 4600 r.p.m. • Dual exhaust system • Fiber-packed mufflers • High-performance 3.42-to-1 rear axle ratio • Top-grain leather interiors • Bucket seats • Matching carpeted luggage compartment • Embossed aluminum side moulding • White sidewall tires • Wheelbase, 123″ • Over-all length, 212″.

Nestle into that foam-cushioned bucket seat!

Slip the smooth, stick-operated Hydra-Matic into "Drive"!

Put your toe to Oldsmobile's exhilarating Starfire Engine!

In an instant you know . . . *this car is unique!* Precision-engineered

—with ultra-high compression, high-speed camshaft,

high-torque rear axle—for the man who thrills to true

sports-car performance, who appreciates custom craftsmanship.

See your Oldsmobile Quality Dealer for complete details.

OLDSMOBILE DIVISION • GENERAL MOTORS CORPORATION

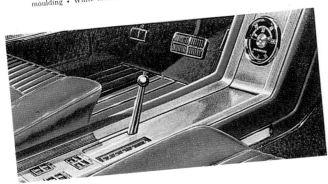

WORSHIP AT ELEVEN AND A HALF PERCENT

"Buy it by the seat of your pants."
—1960 Chrysler Valiant ad

★   ★   ★

Shopping became a second religion for Americans in the 20th century. The new merchandise that flooded from the nation's assembly lines promised spiritual fulfillment, success, and inner peace. Mothers were condemned as immoral for buying the wrong soap for their children, and Hoover vacuum cleaners were bathed in radiant halos of heavenly light. Ad agent Bruce Barton wrote the liturgy of this new consumer religion in his wildly successful 1925 book, *The Man Nobody Knows*, in which he argued Jesus was the first modern businessman!

If consumption was the new religion, the car was both deity and place of worship. The "Rhythmic Ride" of the 1939 Olds acquired new meaning when Norman Vincent Peale thought positively, "When you love a machine and get to know it you will be aware that it has a rhythm. It is in God's rhythm." Roland Barthes claimed, "Cars today are almost the exact equivalent of the great gothic cathedrals; I mean the supreme creation of an era, conceived with passion by unknown artists, and consumed by a whole population which appropriates them as a purely magical object." Future televangelist Robert Schuller would have agreed in 1955. Preaching atop the concession stand of a rented Garden Grove drive-in, the young pastor combined the doctrines of Christianity and consumption for his auto-bound parishioners: "Worship as you are . . . in the family car."

For those not blessed with worldly riches, there still existed a way to buy a little piece of heaven on earth: credit. Installment buying virtually resurrected the auto industry when it was introduced. The Morris Plan banks in 1910 became the first in the country to finance consumers' purchase of cars on credit. By this time the auto industry was facing a danger of market saturation. Most of those who had the cash to buy a car were already driving one. Henry Ford's solution was to continuously lower the cost of his popular car. Those without the cash, unwilling or unable to follow suit, rushed to installment buying plans like gold speculators to California. The Guaranty Securities Company formed in 1915 and quickly became one of the largest financiers of consumers' instant gratification. The General Motors Acceptance Corporation (GMAC) followed on its heels a year later.

Ever conservative, Henry Ford thought such high living was downright immoral. "It has always seemed to me that this putting off the day of payment for anything but permanent improvements was a fundamental mistake," he said in 1915 as he monitored the proverbial crossroads lest some poor sap sell his soul. His cries were to no avail. Once the floodgates opened, millions of cash-poor customers promised, "I'll gladly pay you tomorrow for some steel wheels today." By 1922, over 73 percent of new cars were bought on credit. Ford held out as long as he could but finally created an in-house finance division in 1928. If given the opportunity, Barton would have welcomed the new convert. He had been preaching for some years that credit was based on the Latin word *credo*, to believe. ∎

Purchasing Horsepower
That cool, contemplative expression of the installment buyer. Was she enjoying the inner peace promised in the ads or calculating her monthly payments. GMAC was founded in 1916 to encourage mid-income folks to buy their first car. Years later it still encouraged consumer alchemists to turn "plastic into steel, buying power into horsepower."

New car? Here's why GMAC is the Time Payment Plan so many prefer:

1. GMAC is convenient. Financing for your car, car insurance, even creditor life insurance is taken care of in one simple transaction with the dealer.

2. Terms are arranged to fit your budget and costs are reasonable.

3. Friendly, considerate treatment is yours should financial problems arise.

4. If you move, nationwide GMAC service goes with you through over 300 convenient offices in the United States and Canada.

ASK THE CHEVROLET, PONTIAC, OLDSMOBILE, BUICK OR CADILLAC DEALER WHO OFFERS THE GMAC PLAN

GMAC
GENERAL MOTORS ACCEPTANCE CORPORATION
TIME PAYMENT
PLAN

THRIFTY CAR BUYERS KNOW...
the best way to buy "on time" is to pay down as much as you comfortably can— then pay the balance as soon as you can.

"Next to the church there is no factor in American life that does so much for the morals of the public as does the automobile."
—E.C. Stokes, 1921

★ ★ ★

1960 PLYMOUTH WAGONS (3 series, 9 models)

Even the kids seem quieter

in the wagons built by people who know what parents are up against

1960 DODGE DART WAGONS (2 series, 6 models)

Long before station wagons sported imitation wood paneling, advertisers invented a product called the "family car." E.C. Stokes, former governor of New Jersey, proclaimed in 1921, "Any device that brings the family together as a unit in their pursuit of pleasure is a promoter of good morals and yields a beneficent influence that makes for the good of American civilization. If every family in the land possessed an automobile, family ties would be closer and many of the problems of social unrest would be happily resolved."

The family car appeared as early as 1912 when the Columbus Buggy Company advertised its new electric-powered auto as "The Town Car for All the Family." In a truly democratic appeal, the ad claimed the car was so easy to drive that "a woman or even a child can run it safely." While Mom never doubted her ability, the children were soon relegated to the back seat. Family cars reached maturity in the 1950s and 1960s as little baby boomers graduated from riding in their parents' arms and demanded seats of their own. It was in these years that advertisers crystallized their image of the American family car.

First, the family car was safe. Advertisements chastised parents for endangering their children in cars that did not have the latest safety features. Playing on parents' fear and sense of responsibility, they touted "safety-steel" bodies, child-safety locks, and even air-conditioning as essential to good parenting. Little Junior deserved the best. Pitches directed toward men often argued that the right car could provide family protection even when father was not around to do it himself.

Of course, the family car was also big. Six-, eight-, nine-seat behemoths promised enough room for the whole family (plus luggage) to ride across the country without driving each other crazy. During the baby boom, Ford offered a wagon "built to support any population explosion." As cars got larger so did advertising images of the American family. Grandma and the family dog apparently used to be left at home, but by the mid-1950s large cars meant that they could join

family trips whenever they pleased.

Above all, advertisers claimed that the family car, like many other consumer products, was a key part of a full family life. Dreams could come true if parents took one Buick ad's advice to "Buy Your Family a Friend." A General Motors ad exclaimed, "There's nothing like a new car for healthy, happy family outings!" An ad for the 1978 Plymouth Volare ("the wagon that has America singing") even claimed kids would enjoy packing the rear compartment with 60 bushels of fish! Each of these ads, and many others, claimed the car did more than serve its buyer's needs; it also helped form a family—one that would be lost without it. Similarly, in the process of inventing the "American family car," advertisers went a long way toward inventing the ideal "American family." ■

27 MODELS TO CHOOSE FROM
4 Valiant wagons • 9 Plymouth wagons • 6 Dodge Dart wagons •
4 Dodge wagons • 4 Chrysler wagons

NEW PUSHBUTTON DASH PUTS ALL CONTROLS AT YOUR FINGERTIPS

1960 VALIANT WAGONS (2 series, 4 models)

You can lock all doors from the driver's seat. Great with kids.

No clumsy two-piece tailgate. Rear window rolls down, can be controlled by driver.

Hidden luggage compartment lets you lock valuables safely out of sight.

new wagons from Chrysler Corporation put kids in their place and you at ease.

one thing, there's more room than ever in New Unibody Construction makes body and a solid, welded unit, gets rid of a lot of bulk. nches this saves inside puts added distance en you and your turnpike cowboys.

smooth and quiet ride of these wagons s tensions, too. Chrysler Corporation's ex e Torsion-Aire Ride shrugs off bumps and shock. And Unibody puts a silencer on ks and rattles.

e safety features shown at right also help a relax. You can lock all doors from the 's seat (available in most of our '60 models), ose the rear window from up front, too.

ese wagons built with families in mind, soon.

Quick, the Strong, and the Quiet

n CHRYSLER
ORPORATION

T • PLYMOUTH • DODGE DART • DODGE • DE SOTO
CHRYSLER • IMPERIAL

Family Togetherness
Quality time could be had by all in these spacious 1960 Chrysler wagons. Dr. Benjamin Spock sold millions of books teaching the value of "permissive" child-rearing. These wagons offered to help save parents' sanity in the process.

Look, Kids! Flying Elephants!
Top: Dad cannot seem to find the parking lot as he speeds through Disneyland's pedestrian thoroughfares in his stylish 1956 tri-tone Nash. The theme park, opened in 1955, offered a Snow White version of America deemed appropriate for the whole family. Walt Disney explained, "I hate to see downbeat pictures. . . . I know life isn't that way, and I don't want anyone telling me it is."

Safety Pitch
Right: Safety was often used to sell the family car, as in this 1934 ad. During the Great Depression the loose spending of the 1920s gave way to what one advertising journal dubbed "consumer constipation." Many ad writers chose the hard-sell, pushing fear rather than luxury and style.

"The first of the more than 2.7 million Americans sacrificed on the altar of automobility," as Clay McShane wrote in *Down the Asphalt Path,* was H. H. Bliss in 1899 when he descended from a tram in New York City as "Cabbie Arthur Smith, driving a new electric vehicle, tried to pass the trolley on its right side." The war between public transportation and the automobile had begun. Bicycles and cars were viewed as decadent playthings and were continually pelted with stones as they dangerously navigated their way through the Lower East Side. Nevertheless, *The New York Times* wrote around 1904 that the benefits of autos far outweighed any downside such as the dangers of speed, pedestrian deaths, and cars racing around public streets.

It seemed that new drivers just couldn't wait to hop into their new automobile and put the pedal to the metal. Not until 1954 did Ford offer an optional safety package including a padded dashboard, seat belts, a collapsible steering column, and safety latches on the doors. At which point Ford discovered that consumers had bought the hype that style outweighs substance and saved their pennies for powerful engines and bigger fins. In spite of its best sales efforts, Ford found safety features to be virtually unsalable in the mid-1950s.

Things changed after 1965 when Ralph Nader's book *Unsafe at Any Speed* hit bookstores. Nader was a lawyer who contended that GM's rear-engined Corvair was an ill-handling and dangerous product. What's more, he claimed GM knew it and had chosen to do nothing about it. For 1965, GM had in fact redesigned the Corvair and had exorcised its worst handling traits.

GM suspected that Ralph Nader may have been on Ford's payroll and hired a detective to follow him. Meanwhile, Nader was making a name for himself as a consumer advocate and wouldn't stop until the Corvair did. He pointed out the connections in the Corvair-assisted death of the son of the general manager of Cadillac, the brain damage of the son of another GM executive, and injuries caused to the niece of Chevrolet's general manager.

GM lost the battle, but Waterloo it was not. They discontinued the Corvair, apologized to Ralph Nader on national TV, and later settled out of court with Nader to the tune of $425,000 for invasion of his privacy.

1963 Corvair Monza
Back in the days when women were "girls," the rear-engine Corvair terrorized the streets. This is the car whose ill-fated drivers were martyred for the cause of requiring safety features by law. Ad copy blared with unfortunate truth, "Here's the compact car that threw the book away!" The Corvair was touted as a youthful car since it handled easily, had an innovative air-cooled, flat-six-cylinder engine made of aluminum, and was very fuel-efficient. In 1976, many car manufacturers gave up making convertibles like this since it was difficult to meet new roof-strength laws.

The result of this skirmish was the Motor Vehicle Safety Act of 1966. It set standards for seat belts, padded dashes, sun screens, dual brakes, bumper heights, dash control knobs that didn't stick out as far, and steering columns that gave upon impact. But most important, Ralph Nader and the Corvair had made safety an issue that manufacturers, consumers, and the government weren't likely to ever ignore again. ■

Decades ahead of its time, the Tucker had fuel injection, a rear engine, and numerous safety features, listed here. The Big Three and the majority of consumers, however, ignored any sort of safety improvements at the time and instead focused on bigger cars and better styling.

Preston Tucker was a potential thorn in the side of the Big Three, and on top of it all, he envisioned his car being manufactured outside of Detroit—in Chicago. His flagrant self-promotion and national tours put Tucker's name on the tongue of many a prospective car buyer.

Tucker raised $25 million to produce his dream car and the War Assets Administration gave Tucker an old B-29 engine plant in Chicago to retool. Just when things were looking up, he was allegedly spied on by other manufacturers, who supposedly fed journalist Drew Pearson scandalous information on Tucker, accusing him of embezzling millions.

Tucker was indicted for fraud by the government since he had delayed production, leaving open the possibility that he had embezzled investors' money. On the day that he might have been convicted, he showed 50 of his advanced autos outside the courthouse. He was acquitted of all charges, but the damage had been done, and his plant closed forever. The Tucker had the largest ad campaign ever, relative to the number of cars built.

Tucker Sets a New Pattern of Safety

125-inch wheel base.
Yet only 5 feet high from road to roof.
150-horsepower rear engine.
In the medium price field.

HOW TUCKER HELPS PREVENT TRAFFIC ACCIDENTS

WHICH ALL MOTORCAR MAKERS ARE COMBATTING

62

63

WILL THE ROAD OF TOMORROW LOOK LIKE THIS? . . . . .

Here's one conception of the Road of Tomorrow, which features elimination of all crossings, electronic traffic controls, multi-lane highways keyed to traffic volume and other innovations permitting high speeds with safety. Years away? Perhaps! But it illustrates how earnestly people are trying to make this world a better, safer, cleaner, happier place in which to work and live.

THE TIRE OF TOMORROW IS HERE TODAY

IT MAY be many years before America has a nation wide highway system like the one above. But tires that are safe at tomorrow's higher speeds are here now. Today's Firestone DeLuxe Champions are setting new performance records on the speedway and on the highway. Recently, Wilbur Shaw averaged 100.34 miles an hour for 500 miles at Indianapolis on stock Firestone DeLuxe Champions, just like you can buy at all Firestone dealer stores or Firestone stores. Firestone DeLuxe Champions stay safer longer because they are built with patented and exclusive features, developed through Firestone research, such as Safti-Lock Gum-Dipped Cord Body, Gear-Grip Tread, Safti-Sured Construction and Vitamic Rubber. And remember, they are the *only* synthetic rubber tires made that are safety-proved on the speedway for your protection on the highway.

Listen to the Voice of Firestone every Monday evening, over N. B. C.

BEST TODAY···
STILL BETTER
TOMORROW

MANY DEPARTMENTS TO SERVE YOU AT YOUR NEARBY FIRESTONE DEALER STORE OR FIRESTONE STORE . . . . .

Tires and Tubes • Recapping and Repairing • Batteries
Spark Plugs • Brake Lining • Auto Supplies
Hardware • Radio Supplies • Housewares
Leather Goods • Farm, Lawn and Garden Supplies
Toys, Games and Books • Clothing • Paints
Recreation Supplies • Wheel Goods

Firestone De Luxe CHAMPION TIRES

CHAPTER SIX

ADVENTURE

Like no other single technological advance, the automobile connected the United States from coast to coast. While trains, planes, telephones, and now computers may have played a vital role in uniting towns, states, and the entire country, the car, once paid for, relied on no centrally located service. While a few stops at the gas station would be in order, drivers needed simply to hop behind the wheel at any time and be hundreds of miles away within hours. Each car was truly a personal unit for mass transportation.

Affordable transportation was the ultimate freedom, but it was not without problems. Gangsters reinforced their car doors with bulletproof iron and used them as getaway cars and for drive-by shootings years before the term came into use. Policeman were forced to purchase their own cars to keep up with the likes of Al Capone's armor-plated McFarland and Bonnie and Clyde's stolen Ford V-8s.

Other car owners used their newfound freedom for a more domestic purpose: colonizing suburbia. While tracts of housing between city and country had already been established with trains and trolleys as the means of transport, the

"America in 1960 is full of a tanned and vigorous people who in twenty years have learned how to have fun. . . . When Americans of 1960 take their two-month vacations, they drive to the great park lands on giant express highways. A two-way skein consists of four 50 miles per hour lanes on each of the outer edges; two pairs of 75 miles per hour lanes, and in the center, two lanes for 100 miles per hour express traffic. Strange? Fantastic? Remember this is the world of 1960!"
—GM's Futurama exhibit at the 1939 World's Fair

automobile and the returning veterans from World War II pioneered suburbia in earnest.

Being out of the congestion of the city offered its own rewards, but car owners' wanderlust still lured them to Vacationland U.S.A. First, the national parks were taken by storm. Cities and parks were connected by highways so weekend travelers could "See the U.S.A. in Your Chevrolet" and catch the patriotic fever by seeing purple mountains' majesties or Old Faithful. The idea of a road trip seized America's imagination. ■

Highway Heaven
At long last, America's systems of highways were beginning to be adequate for the powerful engines put out by Detroit. Although it wasn't until 1956 that President Eisenhower would enact the Federal Highway Act, this 1945 Firestone ad already envisioned a streamlined utopia of connecting highways. The vision expressed in car and tire ads of these fantastic futures helped pave the way to pass road construction legislation.

Hey Tex! Where's the Grand Canyon?
The 1940 Studebaker ads pushed the tourist to "make all your 'seeing America' trips in this good-looking, restful-riding, new 1940 Studebaker Commander."

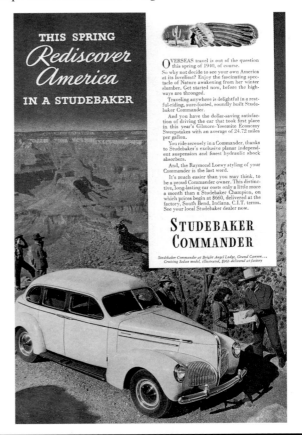

*"It is an urge, irresistible as a tide . . .
to travel, and the ability to travel, has forged a united country,
and reduced a vast area to the dimensions of a community."*
—1952 Budd automobile body ad

★ ★ ★

The 1920s saw the dawn of mass tourism. Until then, long holidays in the country were considered a luxury of the rich. Even the National Park system, which was begun in 1872 with Yellowstone, had been mostly a playground for the few.

As the standard of living rose in the 1920s, more vacationers could afford the train to visit park lodges. The upper crust, meanwhile, turned to the automobile to get away from all the hub-bub. Before 1909, no rural roads were paved, which Packard considered an asset in its 1916 ad for its Twin-6 auto: "Freed—from the confines of city pavements. Liberated—for service on rough country highways and byways."

By 1916, more park visitors came by car than by train. With the Federal Highway Act of 1921 connecting the national parks, distances traveled by car were twice those traveled by train by 1925, and they doubled again in 1929. Even though the car was winning the transportation battle, a 1927 Chrysler 70 ad still compared its "roadability" to trains.

In spite of the "parks for people" movement—meaning parks for car travel—the Grand Hotels in the parks were still not frequented by the majority of travelers. When the not so well-to-do could afford a Ford, they chose the motels that sprang up along major roadways like Route 66. During the Depression, motels prospered as the cheap choice

Motor Lodges: More than 100 Howard Johnson's Motor Lodges in 25 states offer you a sound night's sleep with comfortable surroundings, inviting facilities and Howard Johnson's high standards. Free Teletype® reservation service between all Howard Johnson's Motor Lodges is a welcome convenience.

Restaurants: You know you'll eat well, too, because you can count on good food prepared in over 60 Howard Johnson's Restaurants, and served by you smiling Johnson Girl from an immaculate kitchen. Yo can be sure of Howard Johnson's sensible prices, to

to get out of town. The FBI's outwardly prudish director, J. Edgar Hoover, however, was not a motel fan, claiming that the little cabins were "camouflaged brothels." Then Holiday Inn began spotting the country with green and yellow after getting its start in Memphis in 1952. Other chains of motels like Howard Johnson's soon tagged along.

Now that the country was crisscrossed with highways, tourists no longer needed to exclaim; like a 1922 Daniels ad; "A caravan of camels in the Sahara 'gets you there'—but what an ordeal!" Instead, weekend travelers could act like a 1934 Lincoln ad and "Start out early in the morning, drive five hundred miles, and arrive at your destination so refreshed and relaxed that, if you desire, you can play golf before sundown. . . . Seasoned travelers know best how comfortable and secure the Lincoln is. This car has the power to speed up and cross the Great Smokies. . . ."

The Disneyization of America was taking place, too. Tourists would drive to amusement parks based on European cities and surrounded by vast parking lots. With highways and widening city streets, pedestrians were forced behind the wheel of a car; with Disneyland, people could walk once again through the crowded streets. Sci-fi writer Ray Bradbury was so impressed with Disney's handiwork that he suggested that old Walt Disney run for mayor of Los Angeles to turn the whole city into Disneyland. Vacationing had come full circle. The ultimate tourist vacation spot was representative of what tourists originally tried to escape: the city. ■

Ho-Jo Heaven
These orange and blue hotels either loomed over the road or dotted the sides of highways across the country. In 1951, Charles Kemmons Wilson began franchised Holiday Inns, and emphasized a message of a night with your family, not your mistress, perhaps in response to FBI director J. Edgar Hoover's dim view of motels. Chain motels were preceded by trailers; the first camping trailer was built in 1929 and sold to Henry Ford. Camping fads have swept the country, epitomized by the idealized ultimate American family living out of its mobile home.

the highways

You travel first class at no extra fare

"You Americans really know style"

"Nothing like it abroad"

"Must try that Trigger-Torque Power"

"Ford's our next car"

...in the '55 FORD

Welcome aboard the '55 Ford. It's your passport to the smoothest sailing on the road.

Slip behind the wheel of any of the 16 new body styles. Surround yourself with beauty from the sweeping wrap-around windshield to the flat, ship-shape rear deck. Any Ford you fancy carries the flair of Thunderbird styling from stem to stern—and a score of other new features as well.

Put your foot down—and breeze away in a surge of Ford's Trigger-Torque power. Here's power with far more "wheel push". . . power so alert to safety's demands, that it responds with split-second alacrity. Three new and mighty engines are yours to command: The Y-block V-8; Y-block Special V-8 (available on Fordomatic-equipped Fairlane and Station Wagon models); and the I-block Six . . . the most modern six-cylinder on the road.

Don't mind if heads turn for another look at you. It's the compliment every first-class traveler receives. So don't miss the boat. Drop in at your Ford dealer's this very day!

Treat yourself to a Trigger-Torque Test Drive!

"This could be yours—green knoll, blue skies and all. This could be you, far distant from a world of cares . . . steeped in content. The way's not hard to find in a Chevrolet convertible."
—1950 Chevrolet ad

★ ★ ★

It's a strange irony that the splendor of nature was opened to many only with the development of technology. Long-distance vacations had previously been available only to the well-to-do, but the motorcar made it possible for those of middling income to finally get away from it all (and take a little of it along with them). Thanks to the automobile, millions of motorists, with tent and sleeping bags in tow, took to the hills. They descended in droves upon forests and streams that had recently been accessible only to Yogi, Boo Boo, and their furry friends.

Vacationers could only travel where there were roads to accommodate their new horseless carriages. National parks began admitting auto traffic in 1908, but it was not until the Federal Highway Act of 1921 that auto tourism was encouraged through the creation of a network of quality roads linking the parks. As a result of federal spending that began with the New Deal of the 1930s, navigable roads were extended into the heart of many of the larger national parks. As a result a bitter struggle ensued between preservationists and those promoting increased public access. With the exception of a wartime lull, the next

decades saw the use of national parks skyrocket and the quality of the facilities deteriorate almost as quickly. Fifty-four million people entered the parks in 1954 (the vast majority by automobile) and found 20-year-old facilities designed for a mere 17 million visitors. "The damp night air, heavy with a fall of eye-watering smoke, is cut by the blare of transistor radios, the clatter of pots and pans, the roar of a motorcycle, and the squeals of teenagers," wrote a reporter in 1966. "Except for hundreds of shiny

Land Yacht
These envious ship-goers obviously would prefer traveling in a Ford. While this 1955 Ford may not be direct competition for this ship, many ads showed their cars racing trains, horses, or any other speedy forms of transportation.

Bed on Wheels
With its convertible bed, the 1939 Nash made the nation's outback bearable.

CAMP ANYWHERE! No "hunting up" places to sleep. The roomy rear converts into a full size, soft double bed in five minutes' time...saves $25 to $100 a year for tourists, salesmen.

FAR AWAY PLACES are close in a Nash. The new engine flashes you from 15 to 50 MPH, in 13 seconds flat, in *high* gear.

IT'LL LEAD YOU ASTRAY
—and You'll Like it!

IF YOU'RE RESIGNED to a dull summer on the back-porch swing—better stay away from a Nash.

For here's a car that's not content with just taxiing you to the office and fetching the groceries from town.

It demands a better fate—and so will you.

Look at its clean, windswept lines, and you'll feel it. This Nash is eager to take you to those unspoiled secret places of the world, where roads and hills keep lesser cars away.

There's a little "Weather Eye"* dial that you turn . . . and you stay spotless on the dustiest road...never know chilly drafts. There's a new kind of engine whose pick-up will match any scared jack-rabbit you meet.

There's a *special* gear—a Fourth Speed Forward*—that lets you breeze by the other cars . . .

saves up to 20% on gasoline.

Around and under you are special soundproofing and shock-absorbing features used by no other car-maker . . . so that an extra hundred miles won't jade you.

And there's even a Convertible Bed! So that you can sleep near your favorite trout stream.

We made the windshield wider . . . the gearshift quicker . . . the wheel spin easier . . . the brakes stop faster.

For you're going to drive a Nash like you never drove a car before!

But *why* waste your time reading this ad, when the real thing's down on the corner? Listen—ten models are priced *next to the lowest!* 'Phone your dealer now.

Four Series of Great Cars, 22 Models...10 Priced Next to the Lowest...Delivered at Factory, as Low as $770. Stand. Equipment and Federal Taxes Incl.
(*Optional Equipment—Slight Extra Cost)

$770

Make a change for the Better! This 4-Door Sedan, 117″ wheelbase, is $840 delivered at factory, with standard equipment and federal taxes included. (Whitesidewall tires are optional at extra cost.) 1800 dealers from Maine to California to serve you. *NASH MOTORS DIVISION, Nash-Kelvinator Corporation, Detroit, Michigan.*

AHEAD OF TIME—in styling and in features like the "Weather Eye*," new Nash offers you higher resale value.

It's that New **NASH**
THE CAR EVERYBODY LIKES

Forces of Nature

The 1959 Bel Air offered the perfect way to rough it in the uncrowded outback. While national parks were often crowded beyond capacity, families in ads rarely encountered another soul when they treaded down the paths less taken.

Like all new Chevrolets, this Bel Air 4-Door Sedan offers bigger, safer brakes.

aluminum trailers and multicolored tents squeezed into camping areas, this might be any city after dark."

The most isolated wilderness scenes available to many may have been found in automobile ads. Scores of ads promoted "back to nature" themes, offering the auto as the perfect way to escape the urban rat race and immerse oneself in a plush, green world of wonder. While some parks boasted a population density greater than most city streets, the lucky families in car ads invariably experienced the breathtaking scenery all by themselves. ■

CHEVY'S got the ride and room to go anywhere! This one's _made_ for breaking new trails to fun, with a ride—a Full Coil suspension ride—that makes its foam cushioned seats feel like they're riding on a sunbeam. With handling that keeps you in fingertip contact with Chevrolet's exuberant performance. A spacious trunk that holds picnic gear aplenty. And fashionable Chevrolet style rides poised on a rugged Safety-Girder frame. Your Chevrolet dealer can show you how Chevy fits in with your sort of sport. See him soon!

CHEVROLET THE CAR THAT'S WANTED FOR ALL ITS WORTH • CHEVROLET DIVISION OF GENERAL MOTORS, DETROIT 2, MICHIGAN

This year, **Dodge** is turning up the **fever**

Dodge
CHRYSLER
MOTORS CORPORATION

1969 Dodge Polara. Totally new, it is. Expensive, it isn't.

If you're looking for a big, luxurious new car that sports a low price, look no farther. 1969 Dodge Polara. With such standard items as foam-padded seats, carpeting, and a 230-hp V8. Not to mention an all-new instrument panel and concealed windshield wipers. Why wait, big car lovers? This is your year. 1969 Dodge Polara.

Watch AFL football and the Bob Hope Comedy Specials on NBC-TV.

Nature's Friend, the Automobile

The 1968 Dodge Polaras was as natural as those beautiful flowers surrounding it. How else could it have sprung up in the middle of a field without leaving tire tracks?

Ever-Expanding Cars and Highways

Next page, left: In the early days of the automobile, the main concern of roads was the windrows carved out of the dirt by cars. Then came the slippery brick and the bizarre suggestion of metal roads, which would be unbelievably slick in the rain. When roads began to become "improved roads" and concrete highways, mobilization was truly under way, as even farmers would visit towns on the weekend. (Gambles, Sears Roebuck, and Montgomery Ward decreased mail-order sales and opened variety stores instead.) Not until 1974 would a "proceed slowly" sign be flashed on the automobile when, thanks to the energy crisis, a 55-mile-per-hour speed limit was instituted and some of the Highway Trust Fund money diverted to mass transit.

"On that road the nation is steadily traveling beyond the troubles of this century, constantly heading toward finer tomorrows. The American Road is paved with hope."
—1951 Ford ad

★ ★ ★

In an era when deep-rutted dirt roads meandered from town to town, two men, Dr. Nelson Jackson and Sewall Crocker, crossed the country in a 1903 Winton car. Unheard-of voyages made people envision sci-fi fantasies of coast-to-coast roads, but dreamers still didn't know the composition of these roads. Macadam? Wood? Steel? Debates raged for all three—the turn-of-the-century mentality anticipated endless natural resources—but one thing was clear, dirt roads were necessary as long as most of the vehicles were pulled by horses.

A sea-to-shining-sea highway began with the debut of the first mile of the Lincoln highway in 1914 in Illinois. By 1915, more than a quarter million miles of surfaced roads wound around the United States. The next year saw the Federal Aid Road Act to improve blossoming highways, and in 1921 came the Federal Highway Act to connect all national parks. Soon the first toll road was built exclusively for autos: the Long Island Motor Parkway stretching for 45 miles.

Are they making the turnpikes shorter this year?

Take that next trip in a '61 Plymouth. This Solid Beauty will give you a feeling that roads have never been so smooth, horizons so easy to catch. Everything about this low-price car takes you there in new comfort. It's easy to get in, easy to sit in, easy to see out of. Its quiet one-piece welded Unibody is snug and tight. Its Torsion-Aire suspension (no extra cost) takes practically all the sway and dip out of driving. Plymouth is smoothing the kinks out of the miles. Let your Plymouth dealer show you how.

61 PLYMOUTH...SOLID BEAUTY
A CHRYSLER-ENGINEERED PRODUCT.

Highways as Far as the Eye Can See

Although this seems like an absurd vision of future cities, the number of parking lots around our urban centers ads a touch of truth. This 1948 Futuramic ad is obviously presuburbs with idealistic views of automobile Oz. Ten years later, Robert Young of *Father Knows Best* would be pushing concrete in an advertisement and the resulting 'pleasure trip' from cruising on the "highways [with] the kind of safety every family wants." *Steve Hanson Collection*

GENERAL MOTORS HYDRA-MATIC DRIVE

GM HYDRA-MATIC DRIVE

Hydra-Matic Drive will be offered at extra cost in the Futuramic Oldsmobile "98" and the Dynamic "60" and "70" for '48

400,000 Oldsmobile owners, who drive the Hydra-Matic way, are blazing the trail tomorrow's motorists will follow. They go without shifting—without pushing a clutch—as Hydra-Matic Drive shifts the gears and does the footwork for them. During the past 8 years, these 400,000 Oldsmobile owners have *proved* the day-after-day dependability of GM Hydra-Matic Drive. And today, as Oldsmobile leads the way into a new Golden Era of progress and advancement, Hydra-Matic Drive is still *first* . . . *automatically*

FUTURAMIC OLDSMOBILE

The national focus on highways was not a natural and inevitable course of events; rather it was spurred by the Works Program Administration (WPA), which gave 10 times as much money to improve roads as it did to mass transit. Industry insiders such as GM president Alfred Sloan also helped out by developing the National Highway Users Conference in 1932 to keep the tax on gas going toward highway improvements. Adolf Hitler concurred with this mentality in 1939, saying, "A nation is no longer judged by the length of its railways but by the length of it highways."

Sloan also saw that electric streetcars were crowding the roads with ugly overhead wires and dangerous tracks in the streets that often caught bicycle and car tires. With this argument, deals were struck to dismantle the greatest railroad system on earth. Trains were considered out of date, so the chance for major metropolitan centers—like Minneapolis and Milwaukee—to dump these old beasts in exchange for shiny new buses was as appealing as the trains once had been. Some railroad companies switched to running buses, while GM made a deal with Greyhound for it to exclusively use GM's Yellow Coach buses.

Sloan wasn't the only one pushing the auto agenda, as shown by the work of Frank Lloyd Wright who drew up plans for his "Broadacre City" in 1935. Wright loved cities like Chicago that had elaborate programs to ease traffic through widened streets. His dream city featured elevated highways shadowing the pedestrians down below.

New York City was also the subject of utopian visions that would rid the city of cumbersome sidewalks by installing moving conveyor belts to rush pedestrians on a second layer above the roads. Other proposals involved an overpass above every intersection so impatient cab drivers could go even faster. Instead, sidewalks were merely trimmed back in most major cities, encouraging many people's dreams of a road-filled future.

The real dawn of the highway, however, began in 1956 when President Eisenhower pushed for 40,000 miles of interstate highways. In 1955 he said, "Automobiles mean progress for our country, greater happiness, and greater standards of living." The public dreamed of infinite driving. So "Ike's" decision was extremely popular. The Highway Trust Fund was set up to funnel car and gas taxes toward financing the U.S. highways, the most expensive system of public works ever. ■

SUBURBIA: PRE-FAB UTOPIA

"We shall solve the city problems by leaving the city."
— Henry Ford

★ ★ ★

Henry David Thoreau was the first suburbanite. He chose the quiet nature of Walden Pond for repose while not being able to pull himself from the intrigue of urban Boston; halfway between city and country, he founded suburbia.

While strip malls and ticky-tacky housing developments with lollipop trees can hardly be what Thoreau had imagined, Frank Lloyd Wright might have. Wright created the first "carports" in the 1930s on his "usonian" houses, which were

Pronounced as though spelled, Cry-sler

That was the modest foot-note to the advertisement which appeared December 8th, 1923, announcing the entry of Walter P. Chrysler in the field of automobile manufacture.

The daring which led Chrysler to enter a business already dominated by giants, was reflected in the car he built which bears his name . . . now one of the great names in industry.

After Chrysler came Plymouth and De Soto, and the acquisition of Dodge. We have been suppliers to them for years. Dodge the longest. Budd has made millions of units for steel automobile bodies for all of Chrysler Corporation.

In business, one of the most important satisfactions is the thrill and stimulus of great associations. It is a satisfaction that has been our good fortune to enjoy in generous measure.

The Budd Company, Philadelphia, Detroit, Gary.

Budd
PIONEERS IN BETTER TRANSPORTATION

This Modern World
Taking off from the Frank Lloyd Wright style house and carport, this 1953 Chrysler zooms through the neighborhood. The nostalgic text is juxtaposed with the utopian ultramodern, showing Pontiac's history from factory to founding suburbia.

built specifically for the automobile rather than horses. American architecture turned from the Victorian style of a porch entrance into the front hallway to the suburban model of entering through the garage into the kitchen. The modern driveway with a prominent garage toward the front of the house allowed the fancy automobile to be shown off to the neighbors. Earlier designs for stables always put them behind the house to hide the smell of the horses.

The suburbanization of America was underway, and this 1924 Chevrolet ad thanked the automobile: "The once poor laborer and mechanic now drives to the building operation or construction job in his own car. He is now a capitalist—the owner of a taxable asset. His wages have been increased from $1.50 or $3.00 a day to $5.00 or $15.00 a day. Before or after acquiring the automobile he has begun paying for a suburban home of his own, and is interested in local improvements, consolidated schools, highways, and community service of various kinds. As a *direct* taxpayer, he votes with care and independence. . . . How can Bolshevism flourish in a motorized country having a standard of living and thinking too high to permit the existence of an ignorant, narrow, peasant majority?"

Although the car was created for the success of suburbia, it wasn't until after World War II that it played a leading role. Until then, the suburban lifeline was by rail—trains and streetcars—for which developers often gave money to the center cities to connect their new towns. Since suburbs began as a middle-class phenomenon, the only cars roaring through their streets were often owned by wealthy city dwellers escaping through the suburbs to their country estates.

In the first part of this century, suburbanites hated automobiles since they would speed through their developments stirring up dust and hitting dogs. The police were sympathetic to the suburbs and would often shoot out the tires of speeders rather than try and race after them. Some speed traps even placed rope across the roads to try to halt the cars—until some drivers got ripped out of their cars instead.

These suburbs left houses in the city for blue-collar workers. When Johnny came marching home, he didn't want to live in the squalor of the city, but dreamed of building his own home on a picket-fenced plot. Mass-production of the Model T was the inspiration for developer Abraham Levitt to produce thousands of standardized prefab houses—especially for vets—straight off the factory line for about two-thirds of what a regular house would cost to build. Across the country, identical "planned communities" sprung up as clones of Levittown, New Jersey.

While returning GIs wanted a house first, second on their mind was an auto. Two-car garages became standard for suburban settlements in the mid-1950s. Car sales boomed, as did the baby population. By 1950, a quarter of the population had fled the urban life for suburban sprawl. Today, over half of Americans populate suburbia. While the population had grown by 50 percent, four times as many cars as in the 1950s have hit the streets. Although the car didn't settle suburbia, it definitely expanded it. ■

rmly Established as the Buy of the Year!

THE 870 STATION WAGON

It doesn't take Americans long to recognize a good thing. Look around you at the record-breaking number of Pontiacs on the road.

Notice how Pontiac's exclusive Twin-Streak styling and Vogue Two-Toning set it apart as 1955's most distinctive car.

Get behind the wheel and you'll find that its mighty 180-H.P. Strato-Streak V-8 (200 H.P. with 4-barrel carburetor*) is so nimble and responsive you're on even terms with *any* car on the road.

Its long 122″ or 124″ wheelbase cradles you in the same luxurious comfort enjoyed by those who buy at the top of the price scale. And as for maneuverability and handling, you're right in the sports car class.

And now consider Pontiac's greatest "exclusive"—its unbelievably low price! *You can buy a big, powerful Pontiac for less than many models of the lowest-priced cars!* Visit your Pontiac dealer and drive the automobile buy of the year!

Optional at extra cost.

Pontiac Motor Division of General Motors Corporation

Pontiac leads in station wagon value with four models—the beautiful 860, left, in two- and four-door models, the spectacular 870 four-door and the fabulous Safari.

Pontiac
STRATO-STREAK V-8

Patio and Pontiac
This two-tone turquoise Pontiac shows the neighbors that barbecuing isn't complete without the latest station wagon from Detroit.

Does a Lady ever SLAM the DOOR?

Yes, she certainly does—especially if she's a smart shopper looking at the new cars.

There's no quicker, surer test for sound engineering in car body design —for strong and honest construction —than the sound of a door closing.

Does it make a tinny "plink"? A hollow "bong"? Or does it close against the body with a firm "thud" — a solid, reassuring report of strength and safety?

Make such tests when you look the new cars over. Slam every door, look into each trunk, feel the upholstery and seats. When it's Body by Fisher —you'll be able to *hear* the difference, *feel* the difference, *see* the difference.

When you're "window" shopping—look for plate glass! *Not only those big sweep-back windshields but all glass areas in this magnificent new postwar Body by Fisher are made of safety plate glass. Not just because they are handsomer, stronger — but because you can see so much better, with no dangerous distortion. (P.S. — there's a generous increase in window-space for you to see out of, too!)*

Body by Fisher
— BETTER THAN EVER!

CHAPTER SEVEN

DIVIDE AND CONQUER

"A car for every purse and every purpose."
—1920s GM slogan

The heyday of Ford's Model T could only last so long. By 1924 the price of the "universal car" was only $290, down from a 1909 high of $950. Ford was making a whopping $2 on each new car sold. Such sales represented only 5 percent of the company's profits, the rest coming from growing markets for parts and used cars. Ford faced a problem of severe market saturation, though he was unwilling to admit it. By the mid-1920s, those who were ready and able to afford a Ford had already bought one. The durable auto's seven-year average life and unchanging design discouraged owners from trading in their older models for new ones. At the same time, Ford, whose brilliance lay in production rather than marketing, kept increasing his factories' output of Tin Lizzies. Dealers across the country faced the option of stuffing their showrooms with automobiles they could not sell or allowing the home office to strip away their license to sell Fords. The mass appeal of the Model T had been staggering, but times had changed and Ford failed to change with them.

Two techniques were used to relieve the problem of decreased demand in the 1920s: market segmentation and appeals to new markets. General Motors excelled at the first. Alfred Sloan stepped into the presidency of General Motors in 1923. In the following few years he brought to the automobile industry a new level of marketing sophistication. General Motors shunned the idea of one car satisfying all consumers. Ford's mass-marketed car had run its course and so had marketing to the masses. Sloan offered instead, in the words of GM's famous slogan, "a car for every purse and purpose." With a variety of colors and models, the manufacturer could market different models to different segments of the consumer population.

Other carmakers were quick to follow General Motors' lead. Men and women, old and young, rich and working-class, each found ads addressing them specifically and offering vehicles that supposedly suited their needs and identity. Cars tried to become "as varied as people." To an extent, they did. A black Continental Mark II left observers with a very different impression as it glided down the road than did a hot pink Thunderbird convertible.

At different points of market saturation, the auto industry has tried to solve the problem by appealing to segments of the population that it previously has neglected. Henry Ford made the first such step with the Model T. Before his auto hit the streets, the market for expensive luxury cars had been tapped. Ford sold millions of automobiles by appealing to those who could not previously have afforded a car. Later attempts were made to expand the auto market by pitching to women, teenagers, and people of color. Each case demonstrates the relative conservatism of marketers, for many members of these groups had been owning and enjoying automobiles long before their faces ever appeared in car advertisements. ■

Whoops! How Uncouth!
Detroit desperately tried to lay down the law for female etiquette for the automobile in their ads. Meanwhile, these manufacturers tried to give these women all the luxuries of their suburban tract homes, like heating, air conditioning, plush sofas, and mirrors to check their makeup.

Market Segmentation and the Search for New Markets
Following: Ford offered cars for everyone, from "alert youngsters" to "young newlyweds" to a "capable young executive" to a "man who loves the *sport* of motoring." Which is the car for you?

1. FORD *COUNTRY SEDAN*   2. LINCOLN *PREMIERE*   3. FORD THUNDE[...]

TODAY'S CARS A[...]

Not so many years ago, most of the cars Americans drove were family sedans—tudors and fordors. But just look at the wonderful variety of cars they drive today: the new hardtops, station wagons, convertibles—even convertible hardtops.

And more and more of today's people are choosing these body styles from the Ford Family of Fine Cars. For this whole line is one long parade of car usefulness and style: a shining array of Fords, Thunderbirds, Mercurys, Lincolns and Continentals—cars built to suit your every need.

Out of Ford's endless drive into the future has com[...] *widest range* of cars on the American Road today—all th[...] from the universal Ford to the incomparable Continental.

They are as varied as people. There's a whole new r[...] hardtops, twelve in all (including two new 4-door hard[...] There are four handsome convertibles, including the [...] Sunliner, most popular on the American Road. There ar[...] station wagons (Ford sells more than any other manufac[...] And—there are the Thunderbird and the Continental.

4. MERCURY *MONTCLAIR*   5. CONTINENTAL *MARK II*

S VARIED AS PEOPLE

roughout the line runs the new concept of styling and engi-
g cars to match the people who drive them. You see the
s on any road. Alert youngsters in a Ford (more powerful
the costliest cars of a few years ago). Young newlyweds
Mercury. A capable young executive in his Lincoln. A
who loves the *sport* of motoring—in his Thunderbird. And a

man who loves the classic in car style, in the Continental.

The people are changing—and the progressive trend at Ford
moves faster. You see it every day in the swiftly growing numbers of the Ford Family of Fine Cars on the road. See the final
proof at your dealer's now. Everything that you could want
in a car awaits you there.

THE FORD FAMILY OF FINE CARS   FORD · THUNDERBIRD · MERCURY · LINCOLN · CONTINENTAL

MACHO MOBILES

"Toronado. The all-car car for the all-man man. The line of demarcation is drawn. Men on one side. Boys on the other. Cars fall into place. No question which side Toronado takes. Not with that brawny, broad-shouldered look. And that responsive performance from a 455-cubic-inch Rocket V-8, biggest ever built. And that masterful ride and handling, thanks to the superior traction of FRONT-WHEEL DRIVE and torsion-bar suspension. Like we say, Toronado is all man-right down to that man-sized trunk."
—1968 Oldsmobile Toronado ad

★ ★ ★

"The automobile industry has lost its masculinity," said a horrified GM vice president upon resigning in 1973. Nevertheless, there was no arguing that power was synonymous with virility, and an "obedient" car, as a 1958 Chevy ad acquiesced, proved masculine dominance.

Look at the car- and you know the man likes action

Nowadays, you can tell the man by the car he keeps.

Obviously, the car you see here belongs to a person who likes to go places. And he likes to get there with a minimum of effort and a maximum of pleasure.

We had such a man in mind when the design of this 1955 Lincoln began. And we gave our designers and engineers a goal that we believe has been achieved.

The aim was this: to build a fine car with action to surpass any other car—with beauty to match the tastes of Americans on the move who demand the finest.

Lincoln achieves matchless action with its new Turbo-Drive and new high torque V-8 engine. These two combine to set a new standard for fine-car performance.

Here is a new combination of utter smoothness with ultra quick acceleration. No jerk, no lag—just one unbroken sweep of power from zero to superhighway speed limits.

If you want a car with performance far ahead of its time—a car with beauty that speaks for itself and says so much about your own good taste—the new 1955 Lincoln is for you.

Prove it to yourself with a visit to your Lincoln dealer, to look at a new Lincoln Capri —and to drive one.

LINCOLN DIVISION · FORD MOTOR COMPANY

LINCOLN
for modern living
for magnificent driving

Meeting of... Cadillac Owners!

Through all the higher phases of business and finance and industry, Cadillac is the overwhelming favorite.

It is not at all unusual, in fact, for a fine American corporation to have its entire board membership represented on the Cadillac owner list.

Needless to say, a motor car must offer many wonderful and exceptional qualities in order to win the favor of so distinguished a group of motorists.

And never have these qualities been more clearly evident than they are in today's great Cadillac car.

There is its inspiring beauty, for instance . . . its magnificent performance . . . its brilliant luxury . . . and its extraordinary operating economy.

Of course, you don't have to be a member of a Board of Directors in order to enjoy a new Cadillac car.

In fact, a Cadillac is actually one of motordom's greatest values—the ideal car, economically, for a very wide group of American motorists.

Why not visit your nearest Cadillac dealer soon—and confirm this for yourself.

CADILLAC MOTOR CAR DIVISION ★ GENERAL MOTORS CORPORATION

Chairman of the Board
To move up in this world, better get a Caddie. Conservative black is best since only rebels like Hank Williams, Sr., and that hip-twistin' Elvis drove pink Cadillacs; flashy was not the image GM wanted for their high-end 1955 mobile.

Prior to the dawn of the automobile age, a frequent male role model was a dapper man with spotless, although often impractical, well-tailored outfits. The prevailing ideal was a man in control of the situation—that is, until his Packard broke down. Around the turn of the century, mechanical ability reached a new height as a masculine trait; gearheads across the land became symbols of macho know-how.

Getting men to drop their starched collars and pick up a wrench and grease up their hands

Fisherman's Friend
In the era of Tony Curtis in *Some Like It Hot*, the yachting man off the island of Capri (or in his Lincoln Capri) fought the eternal battle of man against nature. Like *The Old Man and the Sea*, except this time the fisherman wins and puts his trophy on the wall. The 1955 Lincoln was for a man who "likes *action*," while the 1956 Continental was "For the man who knows the secret of being inconspicuously important."

18 GLEAMING FEET OF POWER...
EAGER TO CALL YOU MASTER

THE WINDSOR NEWPORT IN STARDUST BLUE AND CLOUD WHITE

THE NEW *"PowerStyle"* CHRYSLER FOR 1956

You can actually see the thrilling power in this breathtaking new Chrysler.

See it in every fresh, sleek "PowerStyle" line.

See it in the dynamic, pulse-quickening look that says clearly and unmistakably, "Here is the world's greatest performing car!"

And how brilliantly just a few moments behind the wheel bear out that promise. Instantly, you discover a brand-new sense of driving mastery. A new and exciting feeling of complete control never before possible in any car. *You're the boss!*

For here you command the surging power of Chrysler's exclusive airplane-type V-8 engine with the ultra-efficient hemispherical combustion chamber . . . *plus* new Push-button PowerFlite automatic transmission which you control simply by *pushing* a button on the dash! You get a full-time power-assist from Chrysler's new Power-Pilot Steering — a constant, positive, pre-

dictable feel-of-the-road. And you get the safest, most velvety braking with still another "Forward Look" advance — new Power-Smooth Brakes that last twice as long as any others.

We invite you now to enjoy this never-to-be-forgotten experience in driving mastery, and we promise you a new sense of conquest over space. Take your first ride in the magnificent new "PowerStyle" Chrysler. See your Chrysler dealer today!

NOW MORE THAN EVER . . . AMERICA'S MOST SMARTLY DIFFERENT CAR

Master Mobile
The "You're the boss!" pitch probably rang true for many ad men wishing to climb the corporate escalator. Well, at least your 1956 Windsor Newport in Stardust Blue and Cloud White will call you master as you vanish into the happily ever after sunset with your bride grasping on to the window because of the speed of your Hemi V-8 engine in your "PowerStyle" Chrysler.

101

Lady Liberty
Once self-starting engines hit the market, women began to snatch up the most powerful engines they could find. The majority of the female buyers were wealthy and mostly interested in long-distance touring. But many hotels wouldn't let women automobilists traveling without a man stay.

was no easy task. The trick? Go the way of a 1917 Liberty ad by aiming the pitch indirectly toward men through women, "If a woman can drive the Liberty without effort—all day and every day—think how the Liberty must respond to a man's control."

Henry Ford took a different tack in focusing his 1920s ads toward women. He figured that women inevitably made up men's minds about purchasing their new Ford, to spite the fact that women officially purchased less than 2 percent of new cars before 1910. To drive home the machinery-as-macho motif, Henry Ford slammed women in a vitriolic moment in 1934, saying, "They do not want to think on mechanical and industrial matters, and, as a matter of fact, do not want to think much about anything." Then he added, in hopes of not losing a market, that his cars were not "too complicated for women to understand."

As women eventually became almost half of the market for Detroit, many pitches, like the 1955 Chrysler Imperial ad, continued to stress the idea that "The car and the man are perfect complements." "Women drivers" were continually bemoaned as the downfall of driving in spite of statistics beginning in 1925 revealing that women were much safer drivers than men.

Car manufacturers had to watch their step not to alienate half of the population and a huge consumer group. Instead of dwelling on the battle of the sexes, many ads simply tried to appeal to male sensibility and desire. One assured that once owned, a 1957 Cadillac "Gives a Man a New Outlook. . . ." Basic insecurities would vanish by possessing the right car, in this case a 1955 Lincoln, since "Nowadays, you can tell the man by the *car* he keeps." A man's car had become the way to judge his character. Detroit apparently thought so. According to a spiel for the 1955 Chrysler, "The Imperial bespeaks power, leadership and good taste. It is designed for the man who is successful and doesn't have to prove it . . . for the man who doesn't seek prestige because he already has it." ■

WOMEN IN THE DRIVERS' SEATS

"The front seat has plenty of room for the great American blond, yourself, and several tons of raccoon coat—as well as a second blonde, if you believe in numbers. Then, if some offensive male decides that he'll go along too, there's a pleasantly remote rumble seat, where he can be placed in cold storage indefinitely."
—1932 New Chevrolet Six ad

★ ★ ★

At the turn of the century, etiquette books advised women to *always* sit in the back seat of an auto, whether her chauffeur or her husband was driving. Ads featured women safely nestled in the rear while the driver, a man, would tame the unruly engine. A limited number of wealthy women soon could afford their own autos, and car manufacturers discovered a new market.

Women were driving before they could vote in most states. The 19th Amendment wasn't law until 1920, years after ads proclaimed the Saxon "The Car Women Like," and the Overland "the ideal woman's car."

Somewhere West of Laramie

SOMEWHERE west of Laramie there's a broncho-busting, steer-roping girl who knows what I'm talking about.

She can tell what a sassy pony, that's a cross between greased lightning and the place where it hits, can do with eleven hundred pounds of steel and action when he's going high, wide and handsome.

The truth is—the Playboy was built for her.

Built for the lass whose face is brown with the sun when the day is done of revel and romp and race.

She loves the cross of the wild and the tame.

There's a savor of links about that car—of laughter and lilt and light—a hint of old loves—and saddle and quirt. It's a brawny thing—yet a graceful thing for the sweep o' the Avenue.

Step into the Playboy when the hour grows dull with things gone dead and stale.

Then start for the land of real living with the spirit of the lass who rides, lean and rangy, into the red horizon of a Wyoming twilight.

JORDAN MOTOR CAR COMPANY, Inc., Cleveland, Ohio

even policemen. If a female driver blew a tire, crowds would gather to watch her change it. Auto clubs refused to let women join for many years, but car manufacturers would not openly advise against women drivers—why lose their fastest-growing market? Instead they ran ads like one for the 1905 Winton, which read "As simple to run as a sewing machine." And the 1901 Toledo steam carriage that's "simplicity of design and construction" was made so "a woman can operate it."

Women were offered primarily electric cars in the 1910s since cars running on gas required cranking the engine and gave off foul-smelling pollution. Electrics were also deemed worthy of women since they were slower and usually had a maximum range of 50 miles. They worked fine on the smooth pavement of city streets. The Electric Vehicle Association of America knew that "Every woman longs to own an Electric. Every woman knows the comfort, convenience and heightened social prestige it gives." Electrics carried the stigma of being a ladies' car and were rarely driven by men, which was one of the reasons they never came into widespread use.

Then Charles F. Kettering developed the "ladies' aid": a self-starter for the 1912 Cadillac. Other makes quickly followed Cadillac's lead. By 1917 Ford was claiming its car was "As easy to operate as a kitchen range."

Whether Ford wanted it or not, women drivers were here to stay. Ads began promoting the second

Many men, however, were not so eager to share the streets, and anti-woman-driver campaigns were the talk of the town in 1909. Men complained that women weren't strong enough, they couldn't concentrate on more than one thing at a time, and they always expected men to give them the right of way. In 1904, *Motor Age* magazine bemoaned the death of chivalry when police in Connecticut were "not satisfied with arresting all the prominent men automobilists for fast driving, hauled in a young woman operator—and fined her too."

Traditional gender roles were slow to die as women were taunted when they drove by men and

car: "A car for her, too!" said Chevy in 1928. The husband's consent raged as an ad pitch, as in the 1924 Chandler ad advising, "If You Really Want Your Wife to Drive—telephone the Chandler dealer. . . ." And a 1947 Chevy ad in which an elated wife exclaims, "Even my husband says I'm a good driver now!"

Women began to drop hubby off at work—or to "drive the family provider to and from the station" (1922 Chevy ad)—and then head out on the town. Ford had other ideas. In 1924 Ford suggested the car could help mom "contribute to the daily life of her children," but that it also "enables her to conserve minutes, to expedite her affairs, to widen the scope of her activities." *The New York Times*, however, warned in 1912 that, "Any nerve specialist will tell you auto riding has a sad effect on motherhood." Nothing they wrote could stop the revolution; as Chrysler declared in 1936, "Every 5 Minutes a Woman Buys a Plymouth." ∎

Cultured Women Drive Packards

The "fine ladies" market made car manufacturers add vanity mirrors, heat, the self-starter, and eventually automatic transmission and air conditioning. But as a 1923 Paige ad claimed, "She knows little—nor need she—of the lifetime care and conscience engineers have dedicated to the nice simplicities of mechanism about her. Enough that all her motoring whims are gratified—that every comfort serves and surrounds her."

The Dietrich Convertible Sedan

CULTURED women instinctively recognize and appreciate fine work—whether it be the decorator's, the modiste's or the motor car designer's.

The preference such women have shown for Packard cars—not in a few large centers only but in every section of the Union—is a tribute to three particularly well recognized Packard qualities, beauty, prestige and long life.

For women wish the family car and particularly their own private cars to reflect good taste and discrimination inside and out, to possess a distin-guished reputation and, withal, to be of good quality and lasting service.

Woman recognizes a Packard—either Six or Eight—to be something more than a mere utility. She sees it also as a work of art. Here is necessary transportation made luxurious—and clothed with beauty.

The very needlework, and there is much of it hidden in the soft upholstery of a Packard interior, reflects the pride which Packard women take in aiding to produce the best built car in the world.

ASK THE PACKARD MAN WHO OWNS ONE

WOMEN IN THE 1950s: NO LONGER JUST PASSENGERS

"One of the special delights which ladies find in Cadillac ownership is the pleasure of being a passenger. . . . We invite you to visit your dealer soon—with the man of the house—and spend an hour in the passenger seat of a 1959 Cadillac."
—*1959 Cadillac ad*

★　★　★

During the 1950s, women drivers finally began to be commonplace, although ads still recommended consent from their spouses. This was echoed by a 1953 AeroWillys' ad, which confided, "TO UNDERSTANDING HUSBANDS Escort your wife to a Willys' showroom today. We'll do the rest!"

The woman's car, however, was meant not as a gadabout toy, but a functional tool that complemented her daily chores as a housewife; as Chevy advised in 1955, "Every woman needs a *second* love! A busy homemaker . . . and how she travels!

School in the morning, the store, luncheon with friends, the church guild, school again and, perhaps, tea. And what makes hers the best taxi service you ever saw? Her second love—a car of her own." The quintessential woman's itinerary laid out by Chevy.

Women drivers were considered a bizarre anomaly by Detroit advertisers, who were made up entirely of males for many years. Women drivers may have been openly scorned on the streets, locked out of automobile clubs, and legislated against as they were in the 1920s, but they were also the butt of attempted jokes like in a 1962 Corvette ad, which kidded, "Non-mechanical men arise!" and pictured a woman. The same year, Ford ran a TV ad that played off Detroit-perpetuated stereotypes, "Ford cars are so easy to take care of that even my wife can adjust the brakes on our new car. That's the tool she uses [the woman holds up a high heel shoe] Size six and a half brake adjuster."

Ads tried to lure women to buy their wares through style, as with the pitch for the 1955 Ford "Fashion Car." GM's king of design, Harley Earl, credited women with "today's tasteful and eye-appealing colors," perhaps giving them credit for

Commanding Her Car
Ladies always wore pink gloves when behind the wheel of a large automobile, especially when they took charge of a 1952 Mercury. This motif is a break from a 1946 Mercury ad that noted, "Women judge a car mostly on its beauty, comfort, safety, ease of handling, and its perfection of detail." In 1952, it would seem, they preferred power.

Still Trapped in the Back Seat
Etiquette books in the 1920s preached that proper women should always sit in the back even if their husband drove (as opposed to the chauffeur). This 1949 ad keeps the spirit of the delicate female alive with the Joneses enviously peering in the back window. In 1963, Cadillac offered a twist featuring a woman picking up her husband, "Cadillac ladies love to play chauffeur."

the break from the black-only Model T to the multicolored GM special editions. In 1959, DeSoto tried to pitch to women, as well, focusing on fashion and the idea that women are most comfortable in the home: "Being a woman, you'll appreciate DeSoto interiors, too. They're as smartly styled as your own living room."

The break from suburbia and family life was inevitable as long as it involved a car, since "Life was just one diaper after another until Sarah got her new Mustang." When admen saw bra burners, they saw a new market and assumed that the women's lib quest for power meant, of course, horsepower. Ads put words in women's mouths, attempting to egg them on for a 1966 Corvette: "The temptation, you see, was overpowering. They'd had the car a whole week now, and not once had he offered to let her drive. His excuse

was that this, uh, was a big hairy sports car. Too much for a woman to handle. . . . That's why she hid the keys, forcing him to seek public transportation. Sure of his departure, she went to the garage, started the Corvette. . . . His car hard to drive. What propaganda!" While many ads like that gave women the wheel, others backtracked with quips like the 1965 VW ad, which asked, "Does the stick shift scare your wife?"

Pitches for cars in the 1960s sent mixed messages, to say the least. Car manufacturers continued to assume that women's primary goal was wealth, comfort, and power as a 1967 Oldsmobile ad showed, "Next to mink, Toronado is the most exciting animal around. (Who says it's a man's world?)" Even in the 1980s, an Audi ad suggested that women *still* couldn't afford to buy their own cars and were suckers for fur, "Buy Your Wife a Silver Fox by Audi." ■

DOUBLE YOUR PLEASURE: TWO CAR FAMILIES

One of the ways advertisers have tried to expand the market for automobiles is to sell customers more than one. In the 1950s, automobile manufacturers began in earnest to try to sell American families on the idea of owning two cars. Taken to its logical conclusion, this tactic could potentially double car sales without having to convince one devout pedestrian to hop off the pavement and behind the wheel. And think of the neighbors! What would the Joneses think when not one but two steel chassis graced the drive?

The two-car ideal was a way Detroit could sell new cars, but it did double duty relieving a long-term problem of local dealers: the used-car glut. As the car-buying market became saturated and automobiles remained roadworthy for longer periods of time, dealers enticed second- or third-time buyers into purchasing shiny new models by offering attractive trade-in offers on their used cars. This strategy largely succeeded in moving the latest Detroit dreams out the dealers' doors, but

Corralled Without "OK"
The suburbs could be isolating without access to an automobile. Selling the idea of a two-car family was a way that dealers could get out from under all the used cars they had acquired as trade-ins.

Tee-Time Waits For No Man
Buying a second car allowed the man of the house to hit the fairway content with the knowledge that he was the only member of the family being held up by his subpar game. In the 1950s, advertisers began pushing the two-car family ideal as in this 1953 ad from Ford.

left them with a startling number of semi-spoiled cars in need of a new home. In 1922, dealers doubled the number of used cars on their lots from 200,000 to 400,000 units. Trade-ins and used cars were major problems facing salesmen, and unfathomable amounts of energy were expended figuring out how to maximize profits and sales. One early Cadillac sales manual warned that, "The slightest sign of weakening on your part is sure to be observed by your prospect. So you must be as keen to observe any sign of weakening on his part, and when you see it—be quick to utilize it." Such tactics were only mildly successful. By the 1950s, dealers got smart and started pushing used cars as the perfect second automobile for busy families.

Smaller than a Bread Box
The Big Three first faced the foreign compact challenge by importing compacts of their own. They were unwilling to challenge the primacy of their large models (and for a long time most Americans agreed), so they pitched the small autos as perfect second cars. Buyers of this 1968 French Simca could use it to run errands and their first car to tear up the road.

Another pitch for two-car families came when the Big Three started to import their own compacts. They each offered foreign-made compacts under their banners but pushed them as ideal second cars, not substitutes for the requisite Detroit dinosaurs. General Motors had its German Opel, Chrysler its French Simca, and Ford its Taunus from Germany. Each sold rather poorly, but by preaching the benefits of buying a compact as a second car, Detroit could enter the growing small-car market without directly challenging the attraction of their full-size models. ■

Learn the great American sport of Wide-Tracking in a great American sp

Wide-Tracking isn't hard to catch onto, once you've got the right equipment. And five of the most magnificent pieces of equipment around this year, are those bearing the Pontiac Firebird emblem. All five models sport such new excellences as smoother riding rear suspension, upper-level ventilation system (eliminating the need for vent windows) and new stuff under the hood. Choose anything from a 175-hp Firebird to a 330-hp

Firebird 400, each with a bevy of equipment (like padded armrests, front side marker lights) that makes Wide-Track secure than ever. Front-wheel disc brake shift, mag-style wheels and stereo tape the decisions you'll have to make. But thing you'll have to learn is which one of nificent Five Firebirds is for you. Drive a very educational experience.

"PUTTING SOMETHING TOGETHER FOR THE KIDS"

"This is not your father's Oldsmobile."
—1988 Oldsmobile ad

★   ★   ★

Teens and young adults were recognized as an important market segment early in the century. In the 1900s and 1910s amusement parks, dance halls, and certain restaurants began appealing specifically to young consumers. No longer attempting to lure the entire family through their doors, they realized the profit that could be made giving teens a place to be among their own. Manufacturers of clothes, cigarettes, and soft drinks realized in the 1920s that the growing population of college kids had money to burn and could be persuaded to buy products with youth appeal. "No one can afford to overlook a market which is increasing so rapidly in size and importance as the American college market," said one business professor in 1926.

Marketing to young people had three advantages. First, studies showed advertisers that when it came to making buying decisions, children had their parents wrapped around their proverbial fingers. A 1922 ad journalist claimed such kid-power should be used to sell automobiles, adding "a quick pressure on youth is often the best way to get the bigger, slower parent going." In an age in which dating often required an automobile, a "smart" purchase by parents could increase their child's chances of corralling Mister or Miss Right. Second, the young were "embryonic buyers" just waiting to grow up and spend money. In the auto industry, where manufacturer loyalty was relatively high, the attention paid to young consumers could provide the company a lifetime customer. Once a Buick man, always a Buick man.

Last, the young were customers themselves. The expense of purchasing a car was, of course, far higher than buying a soda. It was not until many Americans enjoyed a disposable income in the 1950s that the youth market blossomed and advertisers began regularly pushing automobiles to teens. Speed, power, and styling ruled the day. Perhaps the best example of youth marketing was the introduction of the Mustang in 1964. Lee Iacocca explained that this "pony car" was Ford's attempt "to put something together for the kids." The Mustang sported a 108-inch wheelbase, a floor shifter, and an optional 289-cubic-inch engine. Ford sold half a million in the first 18 months. Unfortunately, this youth-mobile had a built-in aging process. Subsequent models grew wider, longer, and 600 pounds heavier. Such a middle-aged spread left Iacocca to lament "the Mustang was no longer a sleek horse. It was more like a fat pig." ■

Pride of the High School
She may not be a cheerleader but she's got more power than the defensive line in her 330-horsepower Firebird 400. In the 1950s and 1960s, school administrators had to build parking lots to accommodate the hundreds of students who drove cars to school.

Wide-Track 1968 Pontiacs

How Many Miles to Inspiration Point?
The years following World War II found more advertisements with teens behind the wheel. Youth marketing took off just as fast as this stylish foursome in their 1949 Plymouth.

The car that likes to be compared—new Plymouth

The best way to tell new car value is by comparison. Compare the new Plymouth — feature for feature, dollar for dollar, mile for mile — to any car in any price range. Of 22 quality features found in most high-priced cars, low-priced Plymouth has 21 — low-priced car "A" has 13 — low-priced car "B" has 4! For detailed proof, see the new Quality Chart at your Plymouth dealer's now. Then drive "all three" and let the ride decide! PLYMOUTH Division of CHRYSLER CORPORATION, Detroit 31, Michigan

PLYMOUTH BUILDS GREAT CARS

All in the Family
Advertisers discovered early that children enjoyed huge influence over their parents' car buying decisions. The 1933 Dodge "8" was exciting enough to elicit a broad grin from daughter yet cheap enough to give her the serene assurance that father knows best.

SHE: THIS IS THE LOVELIEST CAR I'VE EVER KNOWN DAD!

HE: YES YOU COULD'NT HAVE BOUGHT A CAR LIKE IT FOR $3000 THREE YEARS AGO!

It's the car of cars... in a year of values... the new DODGE 8

You'll say, too, that it's the most car for the money you've ever seen. No matter what kind of car you've been used to driving, this sensational new Dodge "8" will be a revelation to you. People who have owned as many as 5 Dodges in a row are hailing this new Dodge "8" as the finest car Dodge ever built. ✓ ✓ ✓ Smartness? It's the last word in appearance, with its trim body and its luxurious bandbox interior. It's big . . . it's powerful . . . it's fast. It has everything you'd expect from the finest cars ever made—plus. And yet it is an economical car—to buy, to run—a car for 1933. ✓ ✓ ✓ Every factor of time-tried Dodge dependability is present in this great new Dodge "8" . . . and to it has

been added a brilliant array of new features for comfort, safety, and smooth effortless driving. ✓ ✓ ✓ Floating Power engine mountings . . . silent shifting . . . automatic clutch . . . Mono-piece steel body . . . double-drop bridge type frame and low center of gravity . . . hydraulic brakes and other safety features . . . these are only a few of the details that make the new Dodge "8" a real quality car, an aristocrat from bumper to bumper. ✓ ✓ ✓ The new Dodge "8" is waiting to show you how times have progressed. Go to a nearby Dodge dealer and see this great Dodge "8"—a car you couldn't have bought three years ago for less than $3000—but now offered to you at an amazingly low price.

Dodge "8"
AN ARISTOCRAT FROM BUMPER TO BUMPER

W I T H   F L O A T I N G   P O W E R

"The first, toughest job in America is to try to make it in advertising and be black or Puerto Rican."
—Harry Webber, Young & Rubicam, 1968

★   ★   ★

For the vast majority of the life of the American automobile, U.S. auto ads only had white people in them. People of color were conspicuously absent. Car owners in ads could be men or women, old or young, rich or not-so-rich (there were no poor people in auto ads either), but those presented by advertisers as consumers were typically white. Racial and ethnic minorities were stereotypically cast by advertisers as servants, bellhops, and porters when they were included in the ads at all.

One of the reasons that advertisers did not court African-Americans as potential car buyers is that many of them were not. Even in the 1920s, when new- and used-car sales were booming and 1/10 of the workforce at Ford was black, trade journals agreed that automobile ownership was beyond the reach of most black families. The rise of automobile culture and suburbanization in the 1950s in many ways made the situation worse. Both businesses and whites fled urban centers on newly constructed expressways. Many moved to predominantly white suburbs, leaving high concentrations of African-Americans in crumbling inner cities. Access to both suburban houses and jobs depended on automobile ownership. Thus many African-Americans were trapped within a vicious circle: one could not access many good jobs without a car, and one could not afford a car without a good job.

Another factor contributing to the lack of people of color in auto ads came from racism

Ebony and Automobile
Buick and other auto manufacturers in 1970 began running ads in *Ebony* magazine that featured African-American models. Ad industry integration and American manufacturers' slipping market share both contributed to advertisers' search for new African-American customers.

within the advertising industry itself. Starting in the 1920s, the prototypical adman was seen as an ivy-league-schooled WASP. Religious and ethnic diversification happened more slowly in the ad industry than in most. When agencies did begin hiring in the late 1950s and 1960s, most African-Americans found it difficult to escape the confines of "special markets units" in which black agents were hired to sell to black consumers. The legacy of such segregation continues to this day.

Since the vast majority of those creating auto advertisements were white, representations of African-Americans in the ads often reflected white impressions. This resulted in either stereotyping or omission. It was not until the 1970s that things began to change. More African-Americans found jobs in the ad industry, and advertisers were no longer willing to ignore the buying power of a growing black middle class. As foreign companies began to threaten American manufacturers' dominance of the national market, advertisers began courting black consumers, finally acknowledging a segment of the population that had been buying and driving cars for a long time. ∎

Stereotyped Ads
Stereotypes of black porters and servants were, until the 1970s, the primary representations of African-Americans in automobile advertisements. They were rarely shown as potential customers, but always as admirers of white consumption and style.

Pick a mount with the DE SOTO brand, pardner!

Fireflite 2-door Sportsman in Fiesta Red and White

Choose any car in the De Soto corral, and, pardner, you've got yourself a thoroughbred. From hooded headlamps to upswept tail fins, De Soto Flight Sweep styling is the new shape of motion. New Torsion-Aire ride makes bumpy roads seem like super-highways . . . and super-highways seem like clouds. Add up all the great features of De Soto, and you've got the most exciting car in the world today. Drive a De Soto before you decide on any car. You'll be glad you did. De Soto Division, Chrysler Corporation.

Wide new price range . . . starts close to the lowest!

FIRESWEEP – big-value newcomer for 1957 – priced just above the lowest. 245 hp.

FIREDOME – medium-priced pacemaker – exciting style and performance. 270 hp.

FIREFLITE – high-powered luxury for 1957 – the last word in design and power. 295 hp.

Fireflite convertible in Sunburst Yellow, Tamarack Green

Firesweep Sportsman in Samoa Green

NOSTALGIA

"Ours is the little boy or girl in every one of us that yearns for that shiny new car and those warm memories we grew up with. We found a way to make that dream come true along with value. There is that pot of gold at the end of the rainbow."
— *GM executive*

Two themes have been consistent in car design and advertising: the past and the future. The past is usually splashed with Hollywood's pot of golden light, rewriting history to the satisfaction of the present. Goodness and progress ultimately triumph, landing us where we are today. The future, on the other hand, is usually shaped by an artist's utopian vision of streamlined hovercraft and jet packs. Designers attempt to forge this dream into reality and advertisers promote the resulting cars as the epitome of modernity. Slick, aerodynamic cars are influenced less by actual wind resistance than visions of what our popular culture has deemed is our Jetsons-like future.

Lincoln ads around the turn of the century urged wealthy consumers to believe that their cars were made as instant classics in the spirit of the ancients. Meanwhile, Body by Fisher, GM's official body shop, kept its "Coach" logo as a reminder of both simpler times and that the company has been around since the dawn of the automobile. The goal? Suggesting that Fisher could make state-of-the-art car bodies with old-fashioned quality. Perhaps the logic didn't follow, but sales did.

While the 1950s were nostalgic for the flapper days of the 1920s, the 1960s reminisced for the hard-boiled days of the 1930s. A 1966 Chevy Impala ad featured secret agents in the tradition of Raymond Chandler, and a 1969 Olds Delta 88 Royale ad recreated "a scene from the classic movie" *The Bold and the Beautiful.*

In the 1970s, however, nostalgia became the rage as classic auto shows were commonplace across the country. Detroit didn't hesitate to jump on the commemorative bandwagon by making car seats in the spirit of old coaches with button upholstery. Car names of the turn of the century—such as town car, cabriolet, brougham, estate wagon—were readily recycled.

In the 1990s, GM tried to establish simply that it represented the past through advertising America's "love affair with the automobile." Its ads featured photos of classic gas stations and huge 1950s cars pulling up with giant tail fins. Rather than hark back to a past of horses and buggies or town squares free of motorized vehicles, Detroit could now reflect on the automobile's own history as a true representative of popular culture. ■

Where's Trigger?
Establishing the new Western aesthetic, this denim-clad dude takes time out from rassling steers for a photo op. Although prairie schooners were outdated by the auto, they wouldn't scrape bottom like this extra-low 1957 DeSoto Fireflite when heading across the rough plains.

"All I know is what I read in the Falcon ads."
—Snoopy

★ ★ ★

Celebrities may have got the big bucks for plugging DeSotos on their TV shows, movies, or radio programs, but what about the funnies? Why not slip in some subtle hints to get that new Nash to the younger set with Dick Tracy as the medium? Everyone knows that the most read page in the newspaper is the funnies, making it just wise marketing to have Charlie Brown say, "How can Falcon be priced as much as $505 less than those new compacts?" By now, Charles Schulz has probably had the whole Peanuts gang endorse more products than any other comic book characters ever. He even drew the gang singing, "Happy Birthday to you, Happy Birthday from Falcon . . ." as Schroeder bangs out "Hooked on Beethoven" ad jingles.

Cartoonists weren't always on the company payroll as shown in the Lil Abner comic that continually poked fun at GM by proclaiming, "What's good for General Bullmoose is good for America!" ■

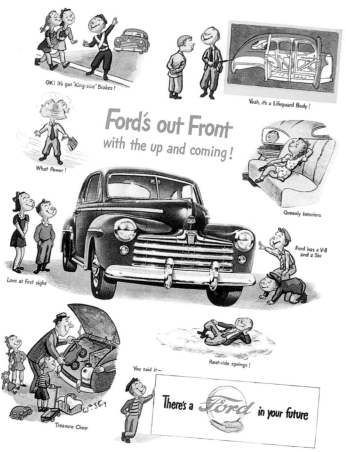

Kids for Ford
The *New Yorker* cartoonist Steig surely got a jingle in his pocket after submitting his characters to the ad biz in this 1947 Ford V-8 advertisement. Ford tended to use the down-home and kitsch quality of comics more often than other manufacturers. *Steve Hanson Collection*

Rambler Comic Compacts
The detective theme comes out again only to find that the bad guys are the big car manufacturers. But hey! This European compact is *too* little. Now the 1958 American Motors' Rambler is *just* right!

The Greek mathematician and inventor, Archimedes, discovered and used many of the principles of mechanical engineering two hundred fifty years B. C.

Early in the 17th Century Galileo pioneered modern astronomy and the measurement of interstellar space.

IN ONE generation automotive engineering has revolutionized civilized life. Yet many of the fundamentals of the science are older than the Christian era.

The spiral bevel gears, which Packard developed and was the first to use commercially, are based on the principle of Archimedes' screw—in use 2,000 years ago. To-day these gears are found in nearly every motor car except the very lowest priced.

They are but one example of the hundreds of advanced steps Packard has pioneered in the 28 years it has held engineering leadership. For Packard engineering no less than Packard beauty of line has been widely imitated.

The greatest achievements of Packard engineers and designers are the new Packard Six and Packard Eight—the finest, the most beautiful and the greatest performing cars Packard has ever built.

PACKARD
ASK THE MAN WHO OWNS ONE

THROUGH the ages men have sought means to avoid the errors of human senses. And little by little science has learned how to replace guesswork by exactness.

Today we may measure the vast distances between the stars and the minute length of light vibrations. Actual measurements as fine as one millionth of an inch are made easily with the light wave equipment in daily use at the Packard factory. The gauges by which many Packard parts are made to fit within one ten-thousandth of an inch must them-selves be constantly checked for still finer accuracy.

So are the latest of scientific achievements put to practical use in the manufacture of the world's best built car.

And Packard is not content to design and build with watch-like accuracy. Precision in manufacture means little if it cannot be easily long maintained in use. The Packard owner can frequently and instantly lubricate all the vital wearing parts *while driving*. Packard precision is protected.

PACKARD
ASK THE MAN WHO OWNS ONE

Pushing the Classics
Archimedes and Galileo stump for the 1928 Packard. This series, which also featured medieval swordsmiths and Alexandrian die cutters, tried to endow Packard with an air of distinction by tracing its development back to the roots of modern science.

While some nostalgic ads looked back to the serene horse-and-buggy days of the 19th century, others took their fascination with the past much further. Looking *way* back, these ads tried to endow their automobiles with the prestige and classicism of ancient Greece or Rome. It may have cost the company precious points in the youth market, but that was apparently a small price to pay to get one's auto into the pantheon of Western achievements. Who could doubt the excellence of an automobile whose design was based on the friezes of the Parthenon or whose die cutters maintained the craft tradition begun by coin makers of Alexander's world empire in 300 BC?

Chrysler took the high ground in a 1929 ad claiming, "Beauty is no chance creation. For the first time in the history of motor car design an authentic system has been devised based upon the canons of ancient classic art." Designers' "search for authentic and harmonious symmetry" led them to the founders of Western civilization. They declared Chrysler fenders were based on "wave border" patterns found in the ancient masterpieces and their grilles reproduced the classy "lotus leaf" favored by early Egyptians. It is questionable whether the car designers were actually dusting off the old art books or whether the avid antiquarians were to be found in the ad agency. In either case, the ad lent Chrysler an air of sophistication that would have eluded it had it limited itself to evoking only the art of, say, the last five centuries.

Other manufacturers shared Chrysler's enchantment with the historical titans. Cadillac and Packard were the most notable. Both companies featured the fathers of Western science in their advertisements with similar results. The quest for stylistic and mechanical distinction led them to make some wild claims about their automobiles' predecessors. It may be impossible to prove that Leonardo da Vinci did not drive the Cadillac in whose ad he appeared, but such a celebrity endorsement carried more weight for some consumers than one by Mary Pickford. ∎

Early Celebrity Endorsement
The bad boys of science are given their due in this 1929 ad. The copy suggests it was a short but revolutionary step from the mathematics of Archimedes to Cadillac's Syncromesh Silent-Shift Transmission.

We can thank these *Ancients* for many of our mechanical marvels *including Motor Cars . . . .*

Archimedes 287-212 B.C. Leonardo da Vinci 1452-1519 Galileo 1564-1642 Stevinus 1548-1620 Newton 1642-1727

WE are inclined to think of motor cars, radios, phonographs and motion pictures as modern inventions. And they are to a large degree. But they could not have been invented had not many fundamental laws in mechanics, engineering and electricity been established long before these devices were ever thought of.

Motor cars are tremendously indebted to the past. Consider, for example, just the transmission.

Many people, not mechanically inclined, would probably say it was like a box of gears. So it is and gears remind us of something we had almost forgotten. It is generally taught when we study elementary physics. It is this:

Every machine can be reduced to a few simple elements, called the Six Mechanical Powers. The primary ones are the lever, inclined plane and pulley. The others, derived from these, are the wheel and axle (derived from the lever)

the wedge and the screw (both derived from the inclined plane).

We are indebted to Archimedes, Galileo, Leonardo da Vinci, Stevinus, Newton and other celebrated mathematicians and scientists of the past for formulating the principles of the six Mechanical Powers and developing their application so that we can use them today in our numerous machines in ways the ancients never dreamed of.

Gears in their operation hark back to the lever principle. And it is common knowledge that gears are one of the oldest methods of power transmission for short distances.

Transmissions have been doing this sort of a job ever since the first car reached the street, but, while there have been many improvements in transmissions during the intervening

years, there was still much to be desired until Cadillac-La Salle engineers developed their new *Syncro-Mesh Silent-Shift Transmission*.

What was particularly needed was a transmission that could fully meet the demands of these days of high speed and congested traffic. That is exactly what Cadillac-La Salle engineers have accomplished. Only a finger touch is necessary. There is no conscious effort, no time lost, no noise. Driving is simpler, easier, safer, more comfortable.

This new transmission is found only in Cadillac and La Salle cars. If you would like to know more about it any Cadillac-La Salle dealer will gladly accommodate you.

CADILLAC MOTOR CAR COMPANY
Division of General Motors
DETROIT, MICH.   OSHAWA, CAN.

CADILLAC-LaSALLE

Lever   Inclined Plane   Pulley   Wheel and Axle   Wedge   Screw

DETROIT GOES WEST

The automobile replaced the horse. Although in many ways the car is a cleaner and easier ride, the public often regretted the change. Nostalgia for the old days of cowboys ran high, so car manufacturers pictured the car as the essential tool to get Tex to the rodeo on time. Cowboys raved in ads about the highfalutin car. "Choose any car in the DeSoto corral, and, pardner, you've got yourself a thoroughbred," read a 1957 ad. Or, "Tie onto this one and you've roped the year's most spirited combination of style and stamina," said a 1957 Pontiac ad.

In the 1920s, cars were forced to compare themselves to the buggy, pointing out that petroleum was cheaper than oats. In the 1950s, with Gene Autry and the gang singing "Rudolph the Red Nosed Reindeer" to millions of new suburbanites dreaming of life on the range, the Big Three had to follow suit. The car had beaten the horse in the transportation race, so why gloat? Instead, car manufacturers could safely remember the supposedly salad days of the Old West. In a typical rodeo ad featuring a 1953 Chevrolet, the ad said "You see *two* pretty exciting kinds of horsepower in our picture up there. One is the rarin', buckin', four-legged kind that makes a rodeo a popular place to go. The other kind is the smooth, quiet horsepower of that spankin' new Chevrolet." ∎

Pontiac's turning a trend into a Stampede*!

It's a Happy Hoe-down!
Cowboys are so excited about the 1957 Pontiac they can't even stay in their stirrups. No more Lone Ranger roaming through ghost towns on Silver, but the 1957 models set a new style for Western cowboys which is inescapable even today. Whether on an Arabian or in an auto, the lone cowhand will get to the Rio Grande.
Steve Hanson Collection

Hey Junior, Get Down!
"Full of spunk . . . but beautifully behaved. . . . It doesn't just *look* sweet, smooth and sassy . . . it is!" brags the ad copy for this 1957 Chevrolet Bel Air. Roy Rogers and Dale Evans had already made the West safe for weekend jaunts, so his little pardners could climb totems free of Indian attacks.

full of spunk...

but beautifully behaved...the '57 Chevy!

It doesn't just <u>look</u> sweet, smooth and sassy . . . it is! And you get sports car control behind the wheel . . . a solid, sure-footed feel on the road, smooth and easy response to every command.

That's why you get more of a lift out of driving a '57 Chevy. Its pep and easy handling make it fun. Safer, too. It's spacious inside, daring in design outside. But still it's a stickler for tradition, and in the grand Chevrolet manner it's known to be as trouble-free as that totem pole!

Drive a new Chevy, one with the exact power you prefer (h.p. goes up to 245*). With triple-turbine Turboglide, too, the newest and smoothest of all automatic drives (an extra-cost option). Your dealer will gladly arrange it. . . . Chevrolet Division of General Motors, Detroit 2, Michigan.

CHEVROLET

1 USA
'57 CHEVROLET

*270-h.p. high-performance V8 also available at extra cost. Also Ramjet fuel injection engines with up to 283 h.p.

The new Bel Air 2-Door Sedan with Body by Fisher—one of 20 new Chevrolets.

"That new V-8 in the '57 Chevrolet is as quiet as a contented cat and as smooth as cream. And it's cat-quick in response when you ask for action! No household tabby sitting in a sunny window ever purred more softly than Chevy's new V-8 engine. . . . It's sassy, sure—but as tame to your touch as a purring pussycat."
—1957 Chevrolet ad

★   ★   ★

Around the turn of the century, ads constantly compared cars to horses. "Horseless carriages" they were called with the motor in the rear to point out the missing horse in front. A 1928 Packard ad followed the equestrian theme, showing to the world that the car was more than a plaything, a car was a tool of good taste. The ad pictured a man advising his son, "A fine car appeals to me as much as a good horse."

Soon, the Mobil red Pegasus zooming through the air reinforced many car ads premise that "Riding is like Flying" as an Essex Supersix claimed in 1927. Later, car manufacturers would go beyond comparing themselves only in print to winged creatures, and begin adding tail fins and other tools of flight to show consumers that autos really are similar to airplanes.

Once the automobile made the horse obsolete, ads began comparing cars to different swift and agile creatures. A 1934 Chrysler ad claimed that, "You have only to look at a dolphin, a gull, or a greyhound to appreciate the rightness of the tapering, flowing contour of the new Airflow Chrysler." Later, a 1949 Hillman Minx ad likened itself to other creatures of the wild kingdom: a kangaroo ("she parks in a pocket"), a swan ("she cruises serenely at 60 miles per hour"), a camel ("she travels 100 miles on 85 cents worth of gas"), and a raccoon ("she hugs the curves like crazy").

While auto agility may have been the rage in the early part of the century, power dominated the second half. Brute force became the rallying cry of "Ram tough" Dodge trucks trudging through piles of mud. Barracudas, Cobras, Mustangs, Stingrays, Jaguars, and any other dangerous animal also succeeded in planting the seed of machismo in their drivers' minds. Ads seemed to say: own this sports car and you will truly be king of the concrete jungle. ∎

Sweet, smooth and sassy! The dashing new Corvette (left) and the Bel Air Sport Coupe with Body by Fisher (above)—two of 20 beautiful new Chevies.

"Kitten-Quiet and Cream-Smooth"
The Chevy may purr like a kitten, but the Corvette to the left will roar like a lion and bite like a stingray. Puns and alliteration were GM ad copywriters forte for this car that was "Sweet, smooth and sassy!" When the Corvette was introduced in 1954, ads in the *New Yorker* and *Sports Illustrated* dubbed it "America's only true sports car." *Steve Hanson Collection*

CHRYSLER STRAIGHT EIGHTS

DUAL HIGH GEAR PERFORMANCE

GREAT BODY STRENGTH

THE SAFETY
OF PERFECT BALANCE

Elephantine Strength
With a publicity stunt that Tonka Toys would later adopt, this 1931 Chrysler Eight ad plopped a 10,000-pound elephant on the roof in front of awed spectators at Coney Island.

Leader of the Pack
Left: For this 1946 V-8, Ford obviously did heavy market research in the animal kingdom. During the war, most ads by car manufacturers tended to be harsh or tear-jerkers, but always patriotic. Postwar, the euphoria following VE- and VJ-Days translated into pop culture, making advertising themes often sophomoric.

Beary Excited!
1956 Ford ads used a teddy bear to push the safety features on their new "Fordor" Victoria.

PAINTINGS

"Marx made theory,
Lenin applied it with his sense of large-scale social organization. . . .
And Henry Ford made the work of the socialist state possible."
—Diego Rivera,
upon painting a mural at the Detroit Institute of Arts.

★ ★ ★

Artists painted cars onto their canvases as advertisements copied art by featuring paintings of cars in their ads. Some artists went a step further and even painted cars, like Pablo Picasso, who developed camouflage paint-jobs to help hide vehicles during World War II.

The poster art influenced by Toulouse-Lautrec could be seen in the commissioned art of Great Arrow cars of the 1920s. In 1962, ads and art became invariably mixed as Pontiac hired artists Van Kaufman and Arthur Fitzpatrick to paint—and autograph—a series of "Wide-Track Pontiac" ads. These ads continued through 1971 when most other companies had long since given in to the medium of photography.

Pop artists such as Wesselmann, Rauschenberg, and Edward Kienholz borrowed the auto image for their paintings. Fellow pop artist Andy Warhol decided to get paid for his appropriated work by Volkswagen and redo the famous VW "Lemon" ad in his own style. Even surrealist Salvador Dali painted his bizarre vision of Datsun's cars, for a tidy fee, of course. ■

"The Headlights of the Automobile World. . . ."
Russian constructivism ruled with diagonals and cubist visions of The Little Marmon auto of 1927. This eight-cylinder car was dubbed "America's first truly fine small car" decades before the word "compact" or "subcompact" would see the light of day.

"Chrysler Can't Do It"
Read the catchy headline with the hook in the ad copy rebutting any "old petulant, pessimistic cry" against the 1928 Chrysler. But as can be seen in the ultra-utopian drawing with zeppelins, skyscrapers, and cars, Chrysler can do anything.

All Aboard!
This advertising artist copied his contemporary Norman Rockwell in this 1925 Dodge Brothers ad in its nostalgia for the days of trains. Just look at that old timer thinking that trains are still a viable form of transport when the younger set is piling on board the Dodge Special Coach.

DODGE·BROTHERS
SPECIAL
COACH

A recent reduction in price is not the only advantage to be considered.

The Coach protects children against open rear doors. It affords exceptional vision on all sides. It provides an intimate and yet roomy interior.

In the Special type, it carries complete special equipment, including nickeled front and rear bumpers, nickeled radiator shell, steel disc wheels, motometer with lock, rear vision mirror, scuff plates, cowl lights and smart special body striping—a striking closed car value.

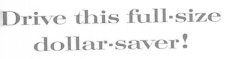

Drive this full-size dollar-saver!

- EXTRA ROOM FOR EXTRA COMFORT!
- A REAL BEAUTY INSIDE AND OUT!
- PERFORMS AS ONLY A ROCKET CAN!

Just try this fashionable, full-size Oldsmobile . . . *and you'll never be satisfied with less!* Here are bigger, higher doors . . . more headroom . . . more legroom . . . plus new Twin-Triangle riding ease and roadability! And Oldsmobile's full-size Rocket Engine delivers instant action on economical *regular* gas! Drive the dollar-saving Dynamic 88 at your Olds Quality Dealer's today!

OLDSMOBILE DIVISION · GENERAL MOTORS CORPORATION

Dynamic 88 OLDSMOBILE
Featuring FASHION-LINE DESIGN... *Rocket* PERFORMANCE!

Museum Hopping
Perhaps wanting us to believe that this work-of-art Oldsmobile had just escaped the Guggenheim, this ad followed a trend during the early 1960s of painting the car rather than photographing it. The logic? Classy paintings meant classy cars, works of art on wheels rather than just pushing all the great qualities of the Rocket 88.

123

HISTORY IS BUNK, BUT I LOVED THE GOOD OL' DAYS

On October 21, 1929, Henry Ford invited President Hoover and Thomas Edison to the inauguration of his tribute to America's past, Greenfield Village. On a 252-acre lot near where he grew up in Dearborn, Michigan, the father of modern production spent over $30 million of his own money to recreate a piece of the idyllic days of yore. The village featured old buildings bought and shipped into the compound from all over the country: Ford's boyhood home, the one-room school house he had attended, the Wright brothers' bicycle shop, the courthouse where Abraham Lincoln practiced. No expense was spared to make Greenfield Village as grand as the world Ford remembered from his youth, sometimes even more so. There was no electricity; gas lamps lined the streets. Evil influences had been scrubbed away; Greenfield Village had no banks, law offices, or saloons. But most interestingly, there were no cars. Guests entered on a steam engine that ran from the parking lot and rode the gravel streets in horse-drawn carriages. Greenfield Village offered a world before speed, before assembly lines, all brought to you by the man that many believed invented both.

Over the years a number of advertisers have shared Ford's romantic fascination with the past. They created surreal images in which their latest models, complete with Futuramic designs, sport around in a world of dandies and southern belles. The schizophrenic ads seems to say two things at once. They nostalgically reflect, "Wasn't it grand way back when?" while at the same time saying, "Wasn't it terrible way back then—look how far we've come." ■

'63 Chevrolet Impala Convertible—Smoothest way to top off a tour of San Francisco

Most comfortable thing since grandmother's lap

Driving ease and creature comfort are the top considerations for most new car buyers. They have a lot of places to travel to, and they want to get there with maximum comfort and minimum effort. That's what you get with any Jet-smooth 1963 Chevrolet, be it a Biscayne, Bel Air, or an Impala like the one in the picture. Chevrolet's Jet-smooth ride whisks you away from home for a weekend, or delivers you briskly to the market in regal splendor never before offered by a car in this class. A look at the *outside* of that crisp, gleaming Body by Fisher assures you of unending comfort and quiet. A turn of the key and a touch of the throttle prove it.

This new Chevrolet is the doggonedest collection of automotive virtues ever assembled under one nameplate. For example, the air-washed flush-and-dry rocker panels, the marvelous system that takes rain water and air from the cowl to rinse away corrosion-causing elements. The Delcotron generator, working quietly and without fuss, to help keep a more-than-ample supply of electrical current on hand and extend the life of your battery. We could go on like this until tomorrow, but really, very little of it will mean much to you, until you drive one. It's a remarkable car, even for Chevrolet Division of General Motors, Detroit 2, Mich.

The make more people depend on

Trolley Beware!
This ad for the 1963 Chevy Impala, "the doggonedest collection of automotive virtues ever assembled," recalls the turn of the century when antisocial, gas-powered buggies threatened the streetcar's dominance of urban roads. The new autos impetuously skittered around the lumbering trains like fleas on an old hound dog. The fleas, of course, took the day.

1968: a vintage year for Wide-Tracking.

In 1959, when our band of engineering experts introduced Wide-Tracking, a good portion of the nation's eyebrows lifted in skepticism. But here it is 1968. And Wide-Tracking makes ordinary cars seem even more so by comparison.

This year, Pontiacs, like that long, luxurious Bonneville below, ride more quietly, more comfortably, more smoothly than ever before. Our habit of introducing revolutionary firsts continues with the world's first bumper that you have to kick to believe. (It's standard equipment on this year's Car of the Year, the GTO.) And our reputation for building great road machines is enhanced every time one of the five Pontiac Firebirds is sent into motion. Which is often.

So when you add it all up, there's really no doubt that '68 Pontiacs will be talked about for years to come. And lucky you. You can own one without paying classic car prices. Just visit your Pontiac dealer.

Wide-Track 1968 Pontiacs

"My, What a Wide-Tracker You Have!"
This dandy takes a break from his barbershop quartet to wow young Miss with the glories of modern automotive engineering, the 1968 Pontiac. She looks impressed, but just wait till she gets a load of Mr. Bell's new invention!

★ ★ ★   ★ ★ ★

GLOSSARY

Ad copywriters don't follow the passé formality of dictionaries; rather they mold the language with superlatives and hyphens that would make Webster roll over in his grave. The more technical and avant-garde the term, the better. Turbo, Torque, and Triple Turbine make consumers drool with lust. Below is a sampling of some of the weirdest terms used to sell cars to America.

Air-Poise Suspension: Special optional suspension on the 1958 Air Borne B-58 Buick for blast-off smoothness.

Auto-Pilot: Now known as "cruise control," "this remarkable engineering device patrols your speed—warns when you go too fast—let's you cruise 'accelerator-free,' " on mid-1950s Chryslers.

Comfort-Aire Ventilation: Airflow system on the 1957 Packard.

Console-Key Instrument Panel: Spiffy dashboard for complete control over the 145-horsepower Super Eight of the 1957 Packard.

Cruise-O-Matic Transmission: Automatic transmission on 1950s Fords.

Dynaflow: Buick's ultrasmooth 1951 contribution to transmission hype.

Econo-master: Gas-saving 90-horsepower engine used in the 1939 Olds.

Flight Sweep Styling: Design of 1957 DeSoto with huge fins, "low silhouette" and lots of headroom.

Flite-Glo Dials: Lighted adjustment knobs on the 1957 Packard to give it the appearance of a plane's cockpit.

Floating Power: Unique, rattle-free engine mounts on 1933 Dodges and Plymouths.

Fluid Drive Simplimatic Transmission: Automatic transmission on the 1940 DeSoto.

Fordismus: German word for Ford's mass production.

Fordizatzia: Russian term for Ford's mass production.

Fordomatic: Ford's automatic transmission with "torque converter smoothness plus the 'GO' of an automatic intermediate gear."

Forward Look: Chrysler's description of its car styling in the 1950s.

Futuramic: Oldsmobile's 1948 solution to the problem of having a car "so new and exciting it requires a new word."

Glide-Ride Suspension: Suspension on 1955 Chevrolets for a "ride in velvety comfort."

Golden Commando V-8: The high-output engine used in the 1958 Plymouth. It was an optional upgrade, yet no one called the standard engine the "tin-foot soldier."

Gyrolator: A "special" fifth chassis spring offered on the 1938 Graham.

Hemi: An engine with hemispherical combustion chambers. A feature popularized by Chrysler.

Highway Pilot: Speed control on the 1966 Thunderbird.

Holiday-type: Rear quarter window that obscures the face of the person in the back seat. Offered by Oldsmobile on their 1951 Rocket 88s.

Hydra-matic Drive: One of the first automatic transmissions available. This particular one was offered with the 1939 Oldsmobile Series 90.

Hydro-Cushion: The suspension system on the 1957 Lincoln.

Jetfire V-8: The 1956 Nash engine that can make "the Rocky Mountains seem Florida-flat."

Miracle Ride: Pitch for the 1958 Air Borne B-58 Buick's supposedly extra smooth suspension for a jet-age blastoff.

Oriflow Ride: Amazing feature of the 1952 Dodge that made even the roughest road feel like ice-skating.

Parlor-Car-that-Flies: Buick's awkward 1941 attempt to describe its smooth ride. Notable because the copywriters openly pine for an English word that means the same but nobly fail to invent one!

PowerFlite Range-Selection: Transmission on 1956 Chryslers.

Prest-O-Justment Seats: "Self"-adjusting seats on the 1957 Packard.

Push-Button Control, Wrinkle-Resistant, Robo Top Convertible Roof: Self-explanatory term on the

1957 Packard, but couldn't save Packard from going out of business five years later.

Quadra-lite Grille: Four-headlight grille available on the 1957 Lincoln to show its "dramatic new beauty" and that "the newness never ends."

Rocket Engine: High-compression engine offered by Oldsmobile in 1950. The only engine that could command the use of "rocket" and "gas-saving" in the same sentence.

R.S.V.P.: "Really Sensational Variable Pitch" propeller blades appearing on the grille of the 1955 Buick.

Safety-Convenience Panel: A mysterious set of controls mounted at the front of the roof on the 1966 Thunderbird that could make one feel like a pilot in a cockpit.

Seat-O-Matic Dial: Feature on the 1956 Mercury that instantly recalled the driver's favorite position for the seat.

SelectShift: An automatic transmission in the 1968 Mustang that could also be shifted manually.

Strato-streak V-8: Engine puff from Pontiac in 1955. One more contribution to the long list of flight metaphors.

Super-Scenic Windshield: Curved windshield on the 1956 Chrysler.

Teletouch Drive: Shift mechanism available exclusively on the 1958 Edsel "lets you shift by a touch at the steering-wheel hub."

Torque-Flight Transmission: Automatic transmission on 1956 Chryslers, also called "TorqueFlite" on DeSotos. Also Torsion-Flight Transmission.

Torsion-Aire Suspension: The 1956 Chryslers and 1957 DeSotos combined torsion bars and outrider springs on their suspension.

Torsion-Level Ride: Suspension on 1956 Packards.

Touch-Down Overdrive: Makes your 1955 Motoramic Chevrolet feel like a jet grinding to a halt at the end of a runway.

Trigger-Torque Power: Catchword for the mighty engine of the mid-1950s Thunderbird.

Triple-Range: Mysterious gadget with questionable function on mid-1950s DeSotos, "Simply touch a button of DeSoto's new Triple-Range push button, and—presto—you're on your way! Positive mechanical control."

Triple-Turbine TurboGlide: Transmission description of the 1956 Chevrolet Bel-Air.

Twin Ultramatic Transmission: Automatic transmission on the 1956 Packards.

Uniscope: A pod above the steering wheel of the 1950 Airflyte model simulating a cockpit.

Venti-Ports: Portholes on 1949 Buicks to give them that ever-desirable airplane appearance.

Weather Eye: Offered as an option on the 1939 Nash. A custom dial that shuts down vents so no fresh air comes into the cab—supposedly no dust or rain either.

★ ★ ★   ★ ★ ★

BIBLIOGRAPHY

Baritz, Loren. *The Good Life: The Meaning of Success for the American Middle Class.* New York: Harper & Row, 1982.

Barnum, P.T. *Barnum's Own Story.* New York: Dover, 1961.

Bayley, Stephen. *Sex, Drink & Fast Cars.* New York: Pantheon, 1986.

Boyer, Paul. *By the Bomb's Early Light: American Thought and Culture at the Dawn of the Atomic Age.* Chapel Hill: University of North Carolina Press, 1985.

Bryson, Bill. *Made in America.* New York: William Morrow & Co., 1994.

Clark, Eric. *The Want Makers: Inside the World of Advertising.* New York: Penguin, 1988.

Finch, Christopher *Highways to Heaven.* New York: Harper Collins, 1992.

Flink, James J. *The Automobile Age.* Cambridge: MIT Press, 1988.

Fox, Stephen. *The Mirror Makers: A History of American Advertising and Its Creators.* New York: Vintage, 1984.

Gramsci, Antonio. *Prison Notebooks.* "Americanism and Fordism."

Hine, Thomas. *Populuxe.* New York: Knopf, 1986.

Hollander, Stanley C. and Richard Germain. *Was There a Pepsi Generation Before Pepsi Discovered It?: Youth-Based Segmentation in Marketing.* Lincolnwood, NTC Business Books, 1992.

Jackson, Kenneth T. *Crabgrass Frontier: The Suburbanization of the United States.* Oxford: Oxford University Press, 1985.

Jung, Carl G., ed. *Man and His Symbols.* New York: Dell, 1964.

Lacey, Robert. *Ford: The Men and the Machine.* Boston: Little, Brown and Company, 1986.

Lears, Jackson. *Fables of Abundance: A Cultural History of Advertising in America.* New York: Basic Books, 1994.

Lynd, Robert S. and Helen Merrill Lynd. *Middletown: A Study in Modern American Culture.* New York: Harcourt Brace, 1929.

Marchand, Roland. *Advertising the American Dream: Making Way for Modernity, 1920–1940.* Berkeley: University of California Press, 1985.

Marinetti, F.T. (Suzanne Brill, translator). *The Futurist Cookbook* (1932). San Francisco: Bedford Arts, 1989.

May, Lary, ed. *Recasting America: Culture and Politics in the Age of the Cold War.* Chicago: University of Chicago Press, 1989.

McLuhan, Marshall. *Understanding Media: The Extensions of Man.* New York: Signet, 1964.

McShane, Clay *Down the Asphalt Path: The Automobile and the American City.* New York: Columbia University Press, 1994.

Meyer, Stephen III. *The Five Dollar Day: Labor Management and Social Control in the Ford Motor Company, 1908-1921.* Albany: State University of New York Press, 1981.

Mitchell, Larry G. *Illustrated AMC Buyer's Guide.* Osceola, Motorbooks International, 1994.

Ortega y Gasset, José. *The Revolt of the Masses.* New York: W.W. Norton, 1932.

Packard, Vance. *The Hidden Persuaders.* New York: David McKay Company, 1957.

Rae, John B. *The American Automobile Industry.* Boston: Twayne Publishers, 1984.

Rothenberg, Randall, *Where the Suckers Moon: An Advertising Story.* New York: Knopf, 1994.

Savan, Leslie. *The Sponsored Life: Ads, TV, and American Culture.* Philadelphia, Temple University Press, 1994.

Sloan, Alfred P., Jr. *My Years with General Motors.* Garden City, Doubleday, 1963.

Stern, Jane and Michael, *Auto Ads.* New York: Random House, 1978.

Tedlow, Richard S. *New and Improved: The Story of Mass Marketing in America.* New York: Basic Books, 1990.

Warhol, Andy. *The Philosophy of Andy Warhol.* San Diego: Harcourt Brace Jovanovich, 1975.

Watkins, Julian Lewis. *100 Greatest Advertisements.* New York: Dover Press, 1959.

Whyte, William H., Jr. *The Organization Man.* Garden City, NY: Doubleday, 1956.

Wilkins, Mike with Ken Smith and Doug Kirby. *New Roadside America.* New York: Fireside Press, 1992.

Wrynn, V. Dennis. *Detroit Goes to War: The American Automobile Industry in World War II.* Osceola: Motorbooks International, 1993.

INDEX